A Frenchman's Duty

A Foot Soldier's Journey

through the First World War

by J. Michael Dumoulin

To those
called to sacrifice
for reasons beyond their full understanding

Third edition

Table of Contents

L'an **mil huit cent quatre-vingt-quatorze**, le Di

à quatre heures cinq minutes du soir par-devant n

Jean Baptiste Branquard , Ad

pour remplir les fonctions d'Officier de l'État-Civil de la ville

cantons, arrondissement de Lille, département du Nord, a

Henri Dumoulin, âgé de vingt sep

Charbon, né et domicilié à Roubaix, le

un enfant du sexe masculin, né la veil

soir, de lui déclarant en a demeure rise

Du Tilleul et de Marie Silvie Mar

six ans, son épouse, ménagère et auquel

voulait donner le prénom de Arthur,

et déclaration ont été faites en présence de

de cinquante six ans, cabaretier et de Augu

de trente neuf ans, tisserand, domiciliés à Ro

du présent acte, nous l'avons signé avec les

témoins.

Dumoulin   Louis Carpentez

Detail, birth certificate, Arthur Dumoulin, 1894

4.

INTRODUCTION

"In the year one thousand eight hundred ninety-four, October 10 at four hours, five minutes in the afternoon, as attested in front of me, Olivier Jean Baptiste Branguard, assistant delegated by the Mayor and assigned the functions of officer of the Registry, town of Roubaix, district of Lille, department of North, in France, in the company of Louise Henri Dumoulin, age twenty-seven, a coal merchant living in Roubaix, presented to me a male child, born the day before at eight in the morning, in his residence downtown on Rue du Eilleul, with his wife Marie Silvie Maryns, age twenty six, housewife, a child whom they have decided to call Arthur."

- *Birth certificate, 1894, Roubaix, France*

This book chronicles four years in the life of Arthur Dumoulin, as transcribed and translated from a journal he kept through the First World War. At the turn of the last century, keeping a personal diary was as normal and natural as posting to a blog is today, although much more private. So, in itself, this story is only as remarkable as the tens of thousands of stories in the diaries of other soldiers who wrote about their experiences in the Great War. What makes this one different, however, is its timeliness as we approach the 100th anniversary of the end of that war, and its perspective from a French foot soldier's point of view. Also, and perhaps more importantly, is the color, insight, and detail added through Arthur's succeeding generations, all career military soldiers. As diaries can be cryptic – especially those written on the battlefield – and include geographic references to places that have been obliterated and vernacular that must be translated across both languages and time, Arthur's story required historic, military, and cultural context. Some of these details come from numerous books, newspaper articles, and, yes, even other soldier diaries, but also from conversations with Arthur as described by his son Charles, a 22-year U.S. military enlisted retiree with combat experience in French Vietnam, Korea, and in the skirmishes that made up the Cold War.

I have two bits of advice for the reader. First, understand that postcards were probably the most popular media during the war. Soldiers had them "pinned up" in the barracks and family members sending news from home to the front bought them, too. Some of the artwork and colorized photos are striking and I've included examples in the book to reinforce points made in the text, but reader beware: many, if not most, postcards produced during the war were printed by both the Allies and the Central Powers as propaganda. And secondly, to any reader compelled to map out every stop along Arthur's journey, my advice is: don't. As I tell my own children "You always have to be some place," Arthur was always some place and he dutifully records all the small villages and communities he visited. Most places are still there but after 100 years of change, including two wars, their names are almost irrelevant. I tried to provide the reader with a sense of distance or setting when it was important but felt that where Arthur went was less important than when and what he did there. Just go with it.

Arthur survived the war, so this story isn't one of those where the hero dies a sad, sudden death at the very end of the book. Arthur was my grandfather and my godfather, and he lived in another country, across eight decades, and two world wars. Although his marriage lasted more than 50 year, so many of his fellow soldiers never had the chance to marry, much less survive France's more than four years of conflict. France alone experienced an estimated 1.3 million casualties. Of the eight million French soldiers who fought in that war, seven million spent time in combat, some in Russia and in Africa, but most along the Western Front. Eight and a half million soldiers on all sides died in the conflict.

France's military casualties included soldiers, sailors, and a new kind of combatant, airmen. The war introduced new and terrifying weapons such as poison gas, the flame thrower, and the tank, which the unprepared, horse-mounted cavalry and entrenched infantrymen on the Western and Eastern Fronts had to adapt to or die.

Arthur's diary records the unimaginable horror in war, but it also reveals the human sides of poise under fire, of duty to family and country, a sense of place, and the challenge of wrestling with demons and keeping them locked away.

-- the author

PART ONE:
FIRST DAYS

To understand Arthur's journal, it isn't really necessary to understand the causes and circumstances that put him in the mud of the trenches, under the explosions of the "obus" shelling from both sides, and in machine gun crossfires. Arthur was in the war to protect France and his family from an invading enemy. Period.

That said, it does help to piece together some of those causes and circumstances to better understand why the French government and France's military leadership so stubbornly held to pre-war fighting doctrine and made fundamental decisions before the war started that ultimately put Arthur in harm's way.

In hindsight, it is almost inconceivable why any country's citizen would blindly follow age-old treaties, political commitments, and inflexible leaders down decision rabbit holes that would almost certainly lead to personal death and the destruction of their city, country, maybe their world. Or is it?

Nineteenth century France was divided into 82 departments, which were administered by 22 different regions, [1] much like counties and states are divided in the United States today. Lille was (and still is) the capital of the Nord-pas-de-calais region, for example, which was (and is) made up of two departments, du Nord and Pas-de-Calais.

In 1871, France lost a six-week war with Prussia, and as a result ceded its eastern-most Fas-Rhin, Haut-Rhin, and Moselle departments to the German Empire. Renamed the Alsace and Lorraine region, it was a prime coal and agriculture producer. But as a result of the Prussian War, France also was forced to give up the city of Strasburg and the pride of the French army,

---

1   *Now 96 departments and 12 regions*

the great fortress of Metz. The combination of losses shook France to its core. Then, in 1882, Prussia, now called Germany, entered into a military treaty with Austria-Hungary and Italy, significantly unbalancing the scales of power in Europe.

In the years after 1882, a vulnerable France turned to its military leaders to develop a work-around strategy that would protect them from an eastern invasion. The best minds in France's military leadership came up with a plan that relied heavily on pre-emptive offensive strikes and battlefield glory and honor. [2] For decades, the doctrine was taught in military classrooms at Ecole de Guerre, France's new military academy, and tactics and maneuvers were hung on the new strategy like Christmas tree ornaments.

At the Ecole de Guerre, military officers were taught an unwavering doctrine of offense at any cost, under any circumstance. It was called the "offensive a outrance." Looking back at the 1871 Prussian conflict, French military theorists believed they'd lost the war because of a defensive mindset. The new offensive approach was spelled out in unambiguous and rigid detail, leaving little room for interpretation. [3] Some of the French Army's battle strategy was brilliantly executed during the opening salvos of Germany's 1914 invasion, but after that, it just happened to be the wrong plan.

By the end of the first decade of the 20th century, France, mostly an agricultural economy, was one of the world's leading trading nations but it trailed well behind both Germany and Great Britain in industrial goods and manufacturing. Germany, although strongly industrial, saw itself as strategically vulnerable, with relatively few colonies to provide the raw materials it would need to grow its manufacturing strength

---

2   *"No Other Law: the French Army and the Doctrine of the Offensive," Charles W. Anders, Jr., RAND Corporation, 1987*

3   *ibid, pg. 12*

or eventually feed its growing population. To protect their unilateral economic interests and national borders, as a counter to Germany's Triple Alliance, France entered into a triple alliance of its own, the "Entente Cordiale" (the "Friendly Understanding"), with Great Britain and Russia.

This, combined with alarm about France's offensive military leanings, made the German government extremely nervous. Paranoia grew inside both alliances. Although Great Britain and France hoped their alliance would help protect their colonial interests, France and Russia were primarily concerned about a German invasion. Belgium and Holland stayed safely neutral, or so they thought.

So, as early as the turn of the first decade of the 20th century, the stage was set, the actors in place, and the script written. All that was needed was for someone to raise the curtain.

Chapter One: Day one

"I leave Roubaix in the company of Paul and Fernand Debruyne. We take the Boulevard de Paris and then the new Boulevard in the direction of Lille. Paul is dragging behind to wait for a few friends and I lose track of him when I arrive at Flers. I go on with some young people I meet, arriving in Lille at 5:15. Just inside the city, at the gate back to Roubaix, I meet Fernand Mesquelier. We go eat at the Grand Place, where I write a few cards and a letter to Céline that I do not mail just yet. We get back on our way to Haubourdin and I find Léon Ghieffry and Bonnart Defryter. We go into an establishment to eat, then search for a place to spend the night but there are so many people that everything is full.

"We lie down under a truck under a door, but we are awakened by the mayor at 10:30. He gives us the order to leave, so we are on our way once again, to Laventie. I lose Fernand Mesquelier between Haubourdin and Fromelles.

"In Fromelles, we pass the French guard posts. The goumiers are patrolling the area and will only let us pass one by one. I regroup with Léon and we resume our journey to Laventie, where we arrive at 4:30 in the morning. We go to Léon's aunt house who welcomes us very nicely and fall asleep in beds that a few Dragoon officers have just left. We wake up at 9 o'clock, feeling a little bit rested. We eat some fries and pâté at 10:30, the first hot meal that we have had since we left."

-- *Diary entry, Arthur Dumoulin, October 9th, 1914*

Mid-morning on Friday, October 9, 1914 the prefect of du Nord-Pas-de-Calais, France's northern-most region, sent out his order. [4] Everyone expected the edict and had been warned to prepare. The prefect, du Nord's equivalent of a U.S. state

---

4   *In 1907, France's federal government decreed that a prefect outranked a commander of an army corps. The legislation, which granted protocol honors higher than those accorded to all but a few at the very top of France's proud and elite list of officers, was considered disrespectful by some career militarists and "a crime" against an officer's sacrifice. (The French War Machine, Shelby Cullom Davis, Unwin Bros, ltd, 1937, pg. 74.)*

cabinet official, ordered the mobilization and evacuation of all men between the ages of 18 and 48. The order, he decreed, was effective immediately and applied to every community from the coastal border town of Gravoline to Fourmies and the farthest villages on the region's eastern border – in other words, the entire area under his jurisdiction. The order required all men to form columns along the Grand Boulevard, a major north-south highway, and march to Lille. All men from Roubaix, just northeast of Lille, and Tourcoing, directly north of Roubaix, were to cross through Lille and head to Haubourdin, a few miles beyond Lille's southern-most suburbs. If they were blocked by high water or German-occupied bridges, they were directed to turn back, but regardless, it was their duty to find a way to set out for Haubourdin at daybreak, or no later than 10am, to enlist. [5]

Germany had invaded neutral Belgium on August 4, three days after declaring war against France, Great Britain, and Russia. Three days after that, an overconfident France advanced into Germany's Alsace and Lorraine regions in a lightning-quick offensive designed to reclaim the territory that they had ceded after the Prussian War. The French Army was repulsed at great cost, and forced to retreat westwards towards Paris, chased by the German 1st and 2nd Armies. Simultaneously, German Army troops occupying Belgium attempted to sweep counterclockwise into northern France in a move designed to quickly take Paris from the north. French authorities had already declared martial law, food rationing, and a general mobilization of troops, [6] but in early September when it became clear that France's pre-war military strategy

---

5   *The Germans occupied Lille five days later, on 13 October 1914 after ten days of road blocks and heavy shelling that destroyed apartments, offices, and homes mostly around the railway station and town center.*

6   *"Mobilization and Adjusting to War," U.S. Consulate in France, https://fr.usembassy.gov/world-war-i-centennial-series-2/*

International News Service post card, "Belgian Soldiers in the Trenches near Malines," unsent. The Battle of Malines (Belgium) in September 1914 was one of the first skirmishes of the war.

13.

could not bring an immediate halt to the invasion, France's government invoked a series of nationwide State of War regulations.

Thanks to a British and French counter-offensive later referred to as the 1st Battle of the Marne, and as a result of a German logistics system stretched too thin too fast, German advances towards Paris eventually stalled at the Aisne River. French and British forces, through a series of successful skirmishes and battles, progressively pushed the German Army slowly northwards towards the North Sea beaches. For Arthur and families in Lille and Roubaix, the war was coming at them closer and closer every day. In fact, it is likely that elements of the French Territorial Brigade traveled through Roubaix and Lille on their way to shore up the British's western flank in Conde, France, and Mons, Belgium.

France at that time was already a conscript nation. In other words, unlike its western neighbor, England, France had compulsory military service. In peacetime, all able-bodied youths on their 20th birthday were obliged to report for at least two, sometimes three years of active military duty. When the Regular French Army failed to push the invading forces back into Belgium in September, the prefect's October draft declaration lowered the age of mandatory service to 18. Dutifully, Arthur Dumoulin left his normally sleepy village of Roubaix that same day. Coincidentally, maybe ironically, it was his 20th birthday.

Roubaix, a mostly rural commune, was but a borough of Lille and the first town in the region that a traveler might have entered as they crossed the Belgium border into France. Roubaix was a border crossing, presumably with the prerequisite guard shacks, passport authority and customs offices, and a few merchants offering goods or services unavailable in the small Flemish boroughs to the north.

The following description is pieced together from

Arthur's diary and recollections of Arthur's stories as told to his son, Charles, with context added from municipal and military documents and historic records of the bombing of Lille between October 9 and 20th.

Arthur left with two of his friends, Fernand and Paul Debruyne. Fernand, 24, and Paul, 19, were the only two male children in a family of seven siblings. The three probably made quite a sight. Arthur was just 168 centimeters (5'6") tall, slightly stocky, with the traditionally thick forearms of his butcher's trade. His straight dark brown hair bounced over bush eyebrows and sparkly-blue eyes. Had the Debruynes, both a half foot taller than Arthur, walked out of Robuaix on either side of Arthur, the three might have personified a sandwich of youthful confidence and bravado.

As days are so often in northern France in October, the temperature was likely chilly but pleasant under a grey sky, looking black in the east, as much, perhaps a harbinger of the coming war as a sign of a pending late morning shower.

The three young men walked down the older sections of Roubaix's Boulevard de Paris and then out along the newer Boulevard south towards Lille. At first, their gait would have been quick and brave, as they were anxious to teach the despised German Kaiser such a lesson that the Prussians, the now despised Boch, would never dare to cross into France again. As with every man, wife or girlfriend, and parent in France, the three friends fully expected to be home by Christmas, or at least by the beginning of Lent, certainly by Easter.

With the German Army approaching, the streets would have been full of people. Many were soon-to-be refugees fleeing before the German army, but a fair number probably were young men like Arthur, some as young as 15 or 16 years old, working their way down the Boulevard, all in the same direction: south. Many of the young men probably carried only

ROUBAIX. – Grande Rue. – rbx3

16.

Roubaix, Grand Rue, pre-war

17.

a rucksack and a hiking stick. Some of them may have had bedrolls tied to the bottom of their backpacks, the rolls of bound fabric beating against the back of their knees in a broken rhythm like shaking cow bells. If refugee lines in more contemporary conflicts are any indication, the migrating crowd certainly would have resembled a herd of cattle, some people walking with their heads down in resignation, apprehension, or fear, and others with their eyes to the horizon, their senses heightened with excitement.

A number of such scenes played out like this concurrently and seemingly extemporaneously across the Nord and its neighboring departments. All along Roubaix's Grand Boulevard, the puddles of pedestrians would have coalesced the closer they got to Lille. Just as streams become rivers, the street corners and intersections would have become like tributaries and eddies of slow-moving people. The stream, however, would have seemed to move purposely southwards, away from the German guns and deeper into France or to the coastal ports, with its steamers and passenger ships.

By afternoon, however, it would have become increasingly clear that approaching Lille from the north would be foolish. Even from a distance, the men would have seen smoke rising from the center of the city and heard the occasional German cannon fire, rolling concussions like thunder off to the west. The men decided to enter Lille through Fleurs, a borough on the city's east side.

At the edge of Fleurs, the Brothers Debruyne decided to wait, perhaps for a classmate or friend who left home later in the day. Arthur pressed on. By the time he arrived in Lille, it's likely that Arthur would have been too distracted by the newness of his adventure or the chaotic preparations unfolding on the streets and squares before him to worry about the Debruynes but he wasn't alone for long. Just inside the Lille city gate, among the flow of pedestrians, Arthur recognized

Fernand Mesquelier, a former classmate from Roubaix, and the two joined as traveling companions.

By dinner time, Arthur and Fernand Mesquelier arrived in the Grand Place, a town square of intersecting roads, its streets leading into and away in all directions like the spokes of a wagon wheel. Fernand and Arthur broke from their group and found a café, perhaps hoping for some bread and maybe hot soup but settling instead for a table to sit and a pair of hard, wooden chairs. With the Germany Army approaching, it is likely that people were beginning to hide their farm stock and hoard firewood: any soup that day probably would have been a little thin and the coffee nearly stone cold.

From a café table, Arthur and Fernand would have curb-side seats to the frenzy in the square: horse-drawn wagons mingling with shiny new motor cars artfully working through the crowd. Suitcases and hat boxes would have been strapped to the hoods and boots of the cars or tied to sideboards of the wagons, with more boxes stacked on passengers' laps.

Under lengthening shadows, Arthur took a moment to write a few cards. He'd probably promised his mother he would do so and starting such a habit on his first day was as likely to cement the practice as anything. Besides, who knew when there would be an opportunity to post another letter. [7] Arthur dropped his envelopes in the mailbox but held onto Celine's, perhaps hoping to add a few lines later about their future together, or tell her how he would miss her, or maybe include some of his thoughts on war. For whatever reason and for the time being, he decided to keep the letter, for now

In early October, the relatively open countryside in the Nord receives twilight well into the evening and the rising of a nearly full moon that night would have given people more time to make their way into Lille's relative shelter. But in the city's

---

7   *Imagine the chaos in a male-dominated French postal service as every able-bodied carrier left to become soldiers.*

narrow cobblestone streets, in the shadow of two- and three-story row houses and tall chimneys, evening falls darker and faster than out in open farmland, and it would have forced visitors and residents alike to move indoors early or work their way to the gas lit side street retreats that still mark the city's signature cafés and restaurants.

The square would have been filling up with people. Judging by the pace and timing of the journal, Fernand and Arthur didn't linger long, taking again to the streets, making their way through Lille, probably anticipating their goal, the induction center in Haubourdin, still miles away.

The two men would have approached Lille's southern cotton mill community about 9:30 in the evening and slipped into one of its many cafés. It's likely that some café owners were serving late into the evening, cooking up what food stock they had left, hoping to make a few more francs to take with them when they closed up shop to flee from the Germans in the morning. With so many miles behind them, Fernand and Arthur would have built up an appetite and the memory of whatever food they were able to purchase – perhaps a roquette and shallot salade or some rillette [8] on fresh bread – would quietly comfort Arthur in the hungriest of times to come. The bread would have been fresh, not crispy and day-old like he preferred, and it would still have been warm: bakers, too, would have been cooking through the night to satisfy the growing crowds of citizen refugees leaving home.

Fernand and Arthur would not have been allowed to linger in the restaurant. Besides, they needed a place to sleep. At that hour, and as transients, and with so many people in the city, finding a bed would have been impossible. Every inn, doorway or café bench would have been full. In their search, despite the darkness and late hour, and much to their surprise

---

8   *Rillette: a kind of "whatever we have" meat spread made up of beef or pork fat, secret family recipe mixes of signature herbs and spices, and a generous amount of salt.*

and pleasure, the two travelers happened upon two classmates, Léon Ghieffry and Bonnaert Defryter. The group set out in search of repose.

Without any better available options, the four friends bedded down underneath a truck or lorry that had been backed under a door overhang, probably to prevent break-ins or looting. Exhausted, no one would have felt like talking.

The men may have been asleep only moments when a man who said he was the mayor roused them. The man was more likely a minor district official, but none-the-less, it's likely the shop owner turned to someone of authority and complained. Nearly midnight, the four youths were soon back in the pedestrian stream of people, all en route to some place, or perhaps just someplace else.

Luckily, Haubourdin was but a few miles away, and a little beyond, Fromelles. But in the dark somewhere between the two villages, Fernand became separated from the others. Perhaps he joined another group of men or simply stopped to sleep, Arthur doesn't say.

Some towns are known for what they grow in the fields or the cheeses and wines they care for in their cellars. Fromelles had always been known for its soldiers, having been a series of stables for messengers that traveled from Paris north to the Belgium border. It is not surprising, then, that in the middle of all of the region's chaos, Fromelles had set up a checkpoint or two. In the pre-dawn hours, Arthur, Bonnart, and Leon approached a guard shack staffed by some French-speaking but obviously foreign irregulars, whom Arthur calls "goumiers." [9] At any other time and at such an awful hour, the group of young men certainly would have seemed suspicious, but seeing no uniforms or weapons, the guards let the men pass the outpost, but only in single file, one at a time.

---

9   The term "goumiers" usually referred to Moroccan Goumiers but was applied as a generic term to African irregulars used in the French and Belgium Flanders region in late 1914. Apparently, real Moroccan Goumiers didn't serve outside of Morocco during WWI.

Not allowed to stop for the night, the three regrouped and set out for the next town, Laventie.

Despite the early hour and the darkness, the road to Laventie would have been alive with cars, mule-drawn carts, and bicycles, some travelers fleeing southwards, some making their way from the south into Lille, intending eventually to head west to Dunkirk or north to German-occupied Belgium ports, hoping to book passage to North Africa, England, or North America. In the early years of the war, traveling was relatively safer at night and the men would have arrived in Laventie around 3:30 in the morning, tired but without incident.

In every village in du Nord, it seems as if everyone is related to someone else and that network of relatives is as practical and functional as the physical roads that connect communities. Arthur Dumoulin's family tended to spread only as far as the countryside south and east of Roubaix, but it was his good fortune that in Laventie, Léon had an aunt, and, apparently, she had a large house. She welcomed the three and offered them warm beds. Despite the early hour, the beds she gave them were still warm indeed: provincial law and the prevailing custom required that private residences give quarters to soldiers if asked.

And so, falling exhausted into a bed that a few uniformed regular Dragoon officers had just left, ended a nearly forty-mile march and Arthur's first day of the war. Leaving from home on a journey through the terrors and glories of a bloody and brutal conflict that was to last for him through 1919, Arthur left as an innocent, taking for granted that each day would lead to the next and that no German bullet could ever touch him. He would arrive home as a man searching for that innocence.

Chapter Two:
Gathering and girding

"We leave Laventie at 11:30 to go to Béthune. Everywhere on the way there we see evacuated people that, like us, are trying to avoid the spiked helmets. We stop to roast some potatoes and eat and after a little rest we follow the Aire Canal up to Béthune where we arrive at 5:30 in the afternoon. We cannot find anywhere to sleep or any place to eat, but we get a pound of bread from the baker, which we share among four people. Soon afterwards, we are ordered by the policemen to leave town right away: there is a big mobilization of machine gun-mounted cars and ammunition convoys moving north. Spahis, Zouaves, and African hunters are waiting to travel into battle. We get out of Béthune and head west a few miles to Annezin where we arrive at 7:30. We gather some hay from haystacks in a meadow and we sleep in a café. In the morning, we return the hay and after a little coffee we get back on the road."

-- October 11, 1914

The next day, duty-bound to reach the induction center as soon as possible, Arthur, Bonnar, Leon, and another, unnamed, traveling companion headed due south out of Laventie. The chaos of frantic traffic clogged the larger arteries so the three took a meandering route on smaller roads. What normally would have been a five-mile walk took the young men all afternoon. Just west of the small village of LaBassee, they ran into the Aire Canal, a man-made commercial waterway connecting the Canal de Neufosse in Aire-sur-la-Lys to the Canal de la Deule in Bauvin. By the time they reached Bethune, they were tired and hungry but Bethune was full of transients. Unlike Lille's refugees and Harbordine and Fromelles' deputized guards, however, Bethune was full of career soldiers, Regulars and units from France's African colonial infantry. All these men, their horses, mules, and military equipment were headed east and north to the front lines.

The Spahis unit that Arthur described was a regiment of French colonial light cavalry recruited primarily from Algeria, Morocco, and Tunisia. Brought up to France from Algeria in August 1914, these were mostly Arab and Berber troops commanded by French officers. The "African Hunters" that Arthur mentions were most likely Arab Berber Zouave soldiers or black "tirailleurs sénégalais," recruited from all of the French possessions in West and Central Africa.

It is probable that a home-spun, small town, new post-teenager like Arthur had rarely seen a French cavalry regular, much less an African one, and even less a black man. His whole life, Arthur would have heard and read about the exotic Foreign Legion and the legendary native soldiers from Senegal and Morocco. He would have been not only intrigued but anticipating being able to describe the site to his brother, parents, and friends, and more than likely he was disappointed when it became apparent that it was prudent for him and his traveling companions to withdraw to Azzezin.

In 1914, two infantry divisions, a brigade of cavalry, a brigade of field artillery (and their horses, of course), and a squadron of non-combatants and trainees made up a regional Corps in the French Army. France had 21 of these, [10] most in France but some in Africa and the Far East. The infantry divisions, where Arthur would eventually be assigned, included 163 regiments of the line, plus 31 battalions of special foot soldiers trained in mountain combat tactics, and 15 regiments and battalions of mainly colonial fighters, including two regiments of the French Foreign Legion. [11]

The foreign foot soldiers, mostly native conscripts from France's West Africa colonies, included the Zouaves; the Turcos from Senegal, also called the Tirailleurs;" and the African Light

Infantry, whom Arthur referred to in his diary as "the African hunters." In all, 450,000 French soldiers through the course of the war came from France's Armee d'Afrique, primarily from France's West African colonies of Algeria, Tunisia, Morocco, Malagasies, Senegal, and Somaila. [12] An additional 150,000 or so "tirailleurs," primarily Senegalese and Vietnamese soldiers, made up France's Armee Coloniale. [13]

Although most of WWI was defined by its terrible use or invention of mechanized mass death, with its millions of casualties from long-range artillery, poison gas, flame throwers, the armored tank, aircraft, and machine gun, in 1914 few of these tools existed. Even though the musket ball ushered in a new era in warfare in 1524, [14] French heavy cavalry wore armor against swords and spears up until 1915, although the helmet quickly came back into universal fashion and use thanks to the obus and machine gun. Generally speaking, however, until the Great War, combat was a "profession of honor," and battles were matches for professional foot soldiers with rifles and swords, mule-drawn artillery, or charging cavalry on horseback.

The French cavalry of WWI wasn't one of tanks, Humvees, and armored personnel carriers. It included 32 regiments of Dragoons, career soldiers similar to the British Royal Dragoons; 21 regiments of Chasseurs, equivalent to British Lancers; 14 regiments of Hussars; 12 regiments of

---

12   "*Colonial Military Participation in Europe (Africa), International Encyclopedia of the First World War, https://encyclopedia.1914-1918-online.net/article/colonial_military_participation_in_europe_africa*

13   "*Morale Among French Colonial Troops on the Western Front During WWI," William Dean, U.S. Air Command and Staff College, Scienctia Militaria, South African Journal of Military Studies, Vol 38, No. 2, 2010, pg. 44*

14   *In 1524, Pierre Terrail, seigneur de Bayard, a French knight eventually known as "the knight without fear and beyond reproach," was mortally wounded in Romagnano, Italy, by a arquebus ball. (The Army of the Future, General Charles de Galle; Hutchinson & Co., London, pg. 56.)*

Detail, French propaganda postcard, "The War, The Zouaves," Series A, No. 3, Simmonds Freres & Clients. Image from unmailed card.

Cuirassiers; and 10 regiments of foreign horsemen from Africa, including mounted "Chasseurs d'Afrique" and their counterparts, the Algerian Spahis. While senior officers were almost always white European continentals, many non-commissioned officers and the mounted Spahis came from "the big tents," a term used to refer to the higher social classes of the Arab and Berber communities. [15]

Colonial soldiers in late 1914, though volunteers, were for the most part combat veterans, many having recently fought in France's newest North African foothold, Morocco. Nevertheless, having been mobilized during Ramadan must have caused this mostly Muslin army some anxiety. Also, their

---

15   *"Morale Among French Colonial Troops on the Western Front During WWI," William Dean, pg 44.*

transition from the more temperate North African climate probably gave them little time to adjust to France's cold and damp weather. Then to add strain onto stress, as these soldiers fought into September and October it became clear that their 19th century weapons – swords and horses – were but blunt truncheons against the new uses of machine guns, field artillery, and trench warfare. Of the 35,000 Algerians and Tunisians who fought during the war, about 20 percent – 6,500 – were killed in the first five months of the war. [16]

From most reports, however, Armee d'Afrique and Armee d'Coloniale troops performed gallantly and bravely, and the French used them as shock troops, entrusting them with some of the most dangerous posts. It is telling that during the troop mutinies in the summer of 1917 (see Part 5), none of the North African units along the front revolted and it was precisely these troops that French leaders used to keep and restore order within its troubled units. [17]

So, as regiments from Africa's finest were working their way north, Arthur and his traveling companions headed for the small town of Annezin, now a suburb of Bethune. Still small by today's standards, covering only about 2.5 square miles in the Pas-de-Calais department west of Bethune, Annezin in 1914 would have been a sleepy, rural community with a single crossroad, a town square, a few shops and cafes, and several brick row houses. It's telling that a café owner would let a handful of strangers, young males with mixed emotions about fighting and adventure, bring in handfuls of hay and bed down in his establishment but perhaps it says more about the pride and integrity of the young men themselves that they carefully replaced a farmer's laboriously-stacked hay the next morning.

---

16   *"Morale Among French Colonial Troops on the Western Front During WWI," William Dean, pg 44.*

17   *ibid*

Chapter Three: On to Chartres

"We depart from Annezin at 6 o'clock in the morning to Marles where we arrive at 9:30. In Marles, a lot of English troops are now arriving by train. We exchange some cigarettes for their cookies, some jelly, and canned beef.

"We find a line of rail cars carrying empty artillery crates back to be refilled with ammunitions. We hop on the back of the trains and jump off just west of St. Pol-Sur-Gernois. On foot, we set out towards St. Pol, stopping to rest in a potato field. There, we burn some dry grass and cook a few potatoes for lunch, adding some beef we traded for with the English. At 2:10, we get back on our way, heading to Warran. Our feet are starting to hurt and our food supplies are quickly decreasing: nobody can help us or give us directions. Above us flies five French planes chasing a Taube [18] that is being fired at by the English. At a road intersection, we come across French and an English policeman who are sorting out the young men passing by. Now with proper directions, we turn right and take the road to Warran, arriving at 5 o'clock in the evening. We cross the village and a small wooded area and take the road to Anvi. Around 7 o'clock we come across a hay stack, and it looks like a great place to spend the night. We have some food left, but not much, and it is not long before we fall asleep but at about 9 o'clock, the hayfield's farmer comes to get us and offers us the shelter of his shepherd's shed. Five of us go to sleep in his farm yard but it is really cold and we can barely sleep. We get up at 4 o'clock just to walk around the shed to warm up, waiting for the morning.

"We leave Warran early, around 4:30. It is foggy and terribly cold. We arrive in Anvin at 5:30 where there are already 300 people in line to catch the train. The taverns are full and we cannot find anything to drink or eat and our provisions are running out. Hungry, at 6:00 in the morning we start walking to Fruges, but at the edge of Anvin we meet up with more than a hundred trucks leaving for a refueling station in St-

---

18   It may actually have been the Austrian-made Taube monoplane, a pre-war aircraft pulled from the battlefield by the German Army in 1915, but the term was applied to almost any German airplane by Allied troops. (https://www.theguardian.com/education/2014/jul/23/first-world-war-slang-glossary)

Omer. One of the drivers of a broken-down truck gives us a little bit of bread. It is wet, almost spoiled, but lacking anything else, we eat it. Nothing to eat between Béthune and Fruges. We walk into Fruges at 9:30 in the morning and stop in a tavern-bakery, where we are able to freshen up for the first time since Laventie. The wonderful citizens in Fruges have made meals in expectation of our arrival and we are really happy to get from them some hot soup and some potatoes. Refreshed somewhat, we walk to the train station intending to catch the 4 o'clock train but there are so many people getting on the train at Anvin that, again, we cannot find seats. With no other choice, we decide to spend the night in Fruges. A man shows us to a house where we could sleep, and since the movies are packed and the Salle de Fête also, we go to the address the man gave us. It is a greenhouse, and the gardener has set the temperature very high. Freeze one night; bake the next! Uncomfortable but tired, we go to bed early, waking up the next day at 4:15. We leave immediately, hoping to be able to get space on the train."

-- October 12, 1914

"At the station, we take seats on the train at 4:30 to be sure we have a place, even though the train does not leave until 8:30. Just before it is time to leave, we meet Jacques and Robert Deschamps and invite them to come with us but they want to leave on a night train. They think that it is safer. Finally, our train leaves Fruges at 8:30 for Calais, and it is packed with people. At Foquenbergues, some very wonderful people give us food and drink, and we arrive in Calais at 2:30, only to leave again at 5 o'clock that night. But in Calais we again meet with Fernand Mesquelier, and catch up with Debruenfer, Fidias, Lepers, Deschamps, Deltombe... and Bonnart, who had reconnected with his girlfriend in Bethune, only to lose her again just before finding us. I still have not seen Paul or Fernand Debruyne and nobody can they tell me where they are. We leave Calais at 5:15 without any news of them and it worries me. At 7 o'clock, we get off the train and eat, and with the cars full when we want to get on, we make our way back to the animal wagons. The train passes Boulogne and

Albeville, then Amiens at 6:00 in the morning. At noon, we eat some provisions that we bought quickly in Calais; pass Cher-Mantes-Vernon; and arrive near Rouen at 5:00 in the evening. We jump off to get more supplies: a loaf of bread and a can of sardines shared again among four people. By 7:00 p.m. we are back on the train and on our way. We pass through Limoges, then through Dreux at 5:00 in the morning, and are in Chartres by 7:30."

-- October 13, 1914

Arthur and his companions took a very circuitous route to Chartres. From Bethune they went almost due west but then at Fruges they suddenly turned north. This would have skirted the fighting taking place about 20 or 30 miles north where the French and British were attempting to establish a front across du Nord to the sea.

The men took the trains north to Calais and then climbed aboard the rear cars, the animal wagons, in order to travel south along the coastline through Boulogne-sur-Mer, across the Coche River, eventually turning southeast to Albeville. Continuing southeast along the north bank of the River Somme for about 20 miles, the animal wagons – with Arthur and his companions inside – would have zig-zagged southeast and southwest, crossing the Seine River but skirting Paris to the east, heading ever deeper into the safer central France countryside. Their destination: Chartres, about 45 miles south of Paris.

It would have been an exciting journey in a fascinating time of change for Arthur, a journey he likely would never have taken on his own. But any fear of what lay hidden in his future would have been assuaged by optimism, determination, and patriotism and any nervousness he might have harbored about change in general would have been quieted by the wonder of all the new inventions and social norms springing up like wild poppies in the first decade of the 20th century.

Motorized trucks traveling alongside mule-drawn wooden wagons. Movie houses competing with opera and theater for night time entertainment. Military automobiles on the roads crossing paths with horse-mounted cavalry. Airplanes! The decade after the turn of the century was one of marvel, juxtaposition, and change. If men could fly, then anything was possible!

While the United States' Wright Brothers are generally credited with the invention of the airplane in 1903, few realize that it took them two more years to build a practical one and that the first air passenger attempt didn't happen until 1908. [19] By 1910, however, machinists and engineers were making and flying heavier-than-air crafts in Hungary, the Netherlands, New Zealand, Canada, Romania, Chile, Poland, Ireland, Belgium, and Switzerland. And, yes, France and Germany. [20] In fact, Germany's Gottlieb Daimler developed the first motor truck in 1896 and introduced the world's first taxi a year later. These new inventions were visible on the roads, in the skies, and in the theaters.

The film industry was born in the 1900s. In fact, although the first feature length, multi-reel movie production came out of Australia in 1906, with the first French projections using the cinematograph as early as 1895, France's film industry was an early world leader by 1910. News of progress and change was there, in the previews and trailers, on the giant screen, in black and white, proof that the 20th Century promised to be like no other. But not everyone was comfortable with the pace or direction "progress" was taking.

Rapid change can produce surprising opportunity, spark new sectors of industry and markets, and generally grow or

19   "Aircraft that Changed the World," Smithsonian Air & Space Magazine, July 2008, https://www.airspacemag.com/history-of-flight/aircraft-that-changed-the-world-45532020/?page=2

20   [20] The Birthplaces of Aviation, Roger A. Mola, Smithsonian Air & Space Magazine, August 2009, https://www.airspacemag.com/history-of-flight/the-birthplaces-of-aviation-35726318/

improve the human condition, but with that change can also come uncertainty in people's long-planned courses of action, challenges and threats to norms and beliefs, and perhaps most powerfully, fear.

To help illustrate this, take the following challenge: think back a decade or perhaps a dozen years and identify the ground-breaking technologies, significant events, and changes in direction of world politics, national alliances, international business and banking, and trade balances. As of this writing, some of the more obvious might be a growing Chinese market, instant digital communication and commerce, small countries with massive nuclear capabilities, and the influence of terrorist organizations like the Taliban and ISES. Less obvious changes with the potential to shape the future might include the emergence of new national space agencies and civilian space lift, a 24 percent reduction in cancer deaths, malicious use of the Internet, unprecedented emigration and migration, and the nationalistic backlash to it across the globe. As you read this in a not-too-distant future time, your list may include a cure for cancer, new countries or empires that span whole continents, or people on Mars.

And then in this exercise, think about your country's military, government, and political strategist, who have on your behalf a responsibility to anticipate and prepare for the impact of such changes. Now, roll back to 100 years ago, back to a European mindset where every country worried about keeping up with new technology and their markets, where Great Britain and Russia were worried about an expanding industrial Germany, and Germany was concerned it could be neither competitive nor nationally secure with only the relatively few colonies it controlled. France, aching for revenge for the loss of honor and territory from the Prussian War three decades earlier, had just adopted an inflexible offensive-at-any-cost military strategy. With all of these changes in play, it's not hard to imagine a Germany that would entertain and justify in its mind a massive first strike.

From Arthur's short 20 years of experience, it's likely that the colorful shades of rights and wrongs of the battle ahead were as black and white as his cinema. Belgium, a neutral state, and France, innocent of any provocation, had been invaded by Germany and if the last war – lost a decade before Arthur was born -- was any indication, cities and villages would be left in ruin and everything that could be stolen would end up in Bavarian storehouses and rich homes in Berlin. Perhaps worse, this time it wouldn't be the eastern Alsace and Lorraine region that would be seceded to the Germans if allowed, but certainly all of Belgium, likely the Nord and Pas-de-Calais departments all the way to the North Sea.

"During the Halt - The Flag," French propaganda post card, Series A, Number 2, 1915

The generation before Arthur's had let Alsace and Lorraine go to the Germans, but in the hearts and minds of the men in Arthur's generation, it wasn't going to happen again, not on their watch.

Chapter Four: Incorporation

"We get some breakfast from the Red Cross but we must keep going on our way to Orleans. At 8:10 in the morning, we leave Chartres. The rail lines and roads are packed, so the trains move very slowly. At noon we stop in Patay where some of us hop off briefly to buy bread and wine. Arriving at Aubais at 2 pm, we pick up some supplies from the Red Cross and are promised we will be able to get more later on the way. We do, in fact, pick up more supplies at Viersoy, where we arrive at 5:15 in the afternoon. We re-board the train, which then passes by Chateau Roux at 7:00 pm and Limoges at 1:25 in the morning. The nights are very cold and we can barely sleep, and unfortunately, we seem to be traveling with a group of trouble makers who steal what they do not need, only to throw it away later. Finally, we arrive at Perigeux on Friday, October 16, at 7 in the morning. It is the end of our terrible trip, but I suspect soon we are going to start a new one.

"At the Périgeux train station, we are brought by four recalled soldiers to a tobacco factory, a big building that looks like a fire station. We join 1160 other people there. After checking in, we stash our bags and packs in a café near the train station, where we freshen up, something we have not done since our departure from Calais. We explore in town, returning to the tobacco factory around noon for lunch but we are told that due to overcrowding we must come back in a few days. To pass the time, I take charge of cooking food for the refugees for the Red Cross and the others help organize a better system of distribution. When not in the kitchen, I walk around town and go to the post office to mail cards to my family that are probably not going to get through. Every night, we report back to our quarters and get some food. We eat around 8:00 every night and we get good nights of sleep on clean hay.

"On the appointed day, I pass the inscription and then the revision council. I am pronounced good for Army service! Immediately, I am taken to the Bugeaud station in Périgeux, where I am billeted on the 4th floor and eat like a real soldier. Shortly afterwards, I'm sent to Chastenez. We now *have to march everywhere. On November 8th, we receive our incorporation papers: I'm to be assigned to the 84th Infantry, now in Terrasson.*

"During my stay at Periguex I find my brother. He has been temporarily assigned to the 1st Army Corps. I leave Périgeux on November 11th for Terrasson where I arrive at 9:00 at night."

By mid-October, Lille had fallen to the Germans and northern France was in full panic. Battles had been fought in their backyard – some literally -- in September and October and refugees were packing into train stations and streaming down dark roads in desperate attempts to move north or south out of the way. Arthur and his traveling companions almost had to fight their way to the induction center but they made it safely and Arthur was "pronounced good" to serve in the Infantry.

Upon acceptance, Arthur would have signed paperwork that committed to pay him a halfpenny a day and a regular allowance of tobacco to serve an unspecified period of time in his country's fight for existence against an invading army.

When Arthur checked in at his first station in Chastenez, he would have been assigned to a squad under the care of a corporal who would have made sure Arthur's hair was cut and deloused. It was the corporal's responsibility to teach Arthur everything about his rifle, and how and to what degree Arthur needed to keep his clothes and bedding clean and in presentable order. His corporal would train Arthur to march, tell him when to get up in the morning, and make sure he was still there for roll call when the lights went out every night. [21]

Training a civilian to become a soldier takes some work. As a butcher, Arthur would have had some experience with a knife, perhaps a shotgun, but neither skill would be much help as he trained to handle a Libel rifle and bayonet.

WWI became the first modern, technical war but in 1914 the French firearm of choice – and issue – was the Lebel

---

21   *The French Army, ex-Trooper, pg. 45*

rifle and bayonet. It was adopted by the French Army in 1886 and had served the military well. French commanders saw no need to replace it, and in their defense warfare technology had indeed changed little between 1886 and 1914. While an automatic rifle was under consideration, the French standard issue bolt action weapon was preferred by military leaders. In their view, a bolt action rifle was more practical: an automatic weapon fired more bullets than its user could carry. [22]

French cavalrymen were issued a straight sword, considered superior to the curved sword carried by the British until the end of 1907; a Lebel carbine; and a bamboo lance. As described by one experienced French soldier and author, "The bravery of French troops is unquestioned, and, in addition to this, the French Army has nothing to learn from the armies of other nations as regards to materiel and equipment." [23]

But a weapon, no matter how accurate or sharp, is only effective when it complements competent leadership, strategy based on facts and accurate intelligence, thorough logistical planning, and teamwork. In peacetime, militaries have the luxury of time to teach an integrated doctrine of such things. In war, especially a war of desperate defensive actions, the conversion of civilian individuals into a cohesive fighting and killing unit must be done quickly. Book work is minimized; daily practical field exercises and practice on the firing range become the norm. Every soldier is quickly exposed to nearly every task. In Arthur's army, line infantrymen were assigned to "fatigue details" and rotated into non-combat duties, such as supply and maintenance. [24] To prepare, basic training would have included learning to drive; how to handle mules; how to butcher, bake, and cook (something Arthur already knew how

---

22   *The French Army, ex-Trooper, pg. 17*

23   *ibid, pg. 17*

24   *"Ratatouille Froid – French Army Rations in WWI," http://17thdivision.tripod.com/ rationsoftheageofempire/id16*

to do); basic first aid, field communications and signals; and eventually how to dig and reinforce trenches, maintain and use a gas mask, and efficiently carry out mortuary duties.

One nearly universal team building method even today is learning to march. This was a practical skill before the advent of troop conveyances such as trains and trucks, yet today's military soldiers, airmen, and sailors are still taught to march. Why? Just as any skilled dancer will tell you that practice helps you get in your partner's head and anticipate their next move, marching coalesces a military unit's mind and body like nothing else.

French soldiers were trained to march "piou-piou," and a shortened version of the word, "poilu," eventually became slang for the French infantryman himself. Roughly translated, piou-piou means "like a baby chicken." It has a very precise cadence that includes 160 short, quick steps per minute, which allows the recruit to cover 3000 yards, with the pace increasing by 1000 yards until, after everyone has warmed up the group can cover 12,000 yards per minute. As the distance increases, so, too, does the length of each step, but eventually the number of steps decreases. To cross a field quickly or to execute a turn in formation, which necessitates one side of the marching column to walk faster than the other, an officer might call for a "double quick" marching pace of up to 180 long steps. In this way, a battalion can cover up to about 40 miles in a days march.[25] Unlike the "smartness" of the marching style of their British infantry counterpart, which was intended to impress potential recruits in Great Britain's voluntary service system, the French infantry of drafted citizen solders could adopt a more leisurely, less rigid style. It was not out of the question, for example, for officers and enlisted alike – yes, officers were expected to lead their units by example – to break rank occasionally to purchase food or drink from passing vendors. [26]

---

25   "The French Army," exTrooper, pg. 23

26   ibid

Detail, colorized photograph postcard, "French Infantry Advancing on the Double Quick," International News Service, NY. Image from card postmarked: May 3, 1915, NY

PART TWO:
TRAINING AND DEPARTURE
TO THE FRONT

Chapter One:
November, 1914 to January, 1915

"When I wake up, I go to the 84th Regiment's building where I was sent to as part of the 1st division. Our class of new recruits is quartered in a school and I and many young people gather for exercise. The people are very good to us who have just arrived. We eat our first mess tin at 10:30. It does not seem so bad: I have not eaten since we snacked at the Bugeaud station in Périguex. I am now the only one left of the people with whom I started traveling since Calais. Gustave Delneufcourt is deferred and leaves to go work at Treysinsae, 18 km from Périgeux. André Deschamps, Bonnart, Léon Fidias, P. Deltombe, J. Lilert are diffusing themselves also. Fern-and Mesquelier joins the war effort in Paris where he will very quickly find something to do. I get all my military supplies and uniforms and I start my training. So far, it does not seem so hard. On Sunday we go to mass and I go out with my new comrades Farvocque and Proven and find some young people from Roubaix. We laugh a lot."

-- Terrasson, November 12, 1914

"A few days later, my brother comes and joins me at the 84th and is assigned to the same division. On the 19th my brother receives his orders and leaves for the 9th Battalion of Chasseurs de Pied. Around December 20th my unit leaves for a camp in Courtine to complete our instruction and training. We stay there for Christmas and New Year. We send letters to our parents but God knows when they will get them."

-- Terrasson, January 2, 1915

Armies, Divisions, Regiments (also called Brigades), Battalions, and Companies: it can all be confusing and hard to keep straight. In Arthur's diary, it's often not clear which unit his generic "we" refers to but his descriptions often provide some clues. Certain tasks, such as taking a machine gun outpost or running a supply depot, are obvious: companies and groups were in the trenches and most supplies were distributed at the company and regiment levels. Officer messes would be where there were groups of officers, probably placed in regiment encampments. General officer messes normally would be wherever the division or Army was headquartered.

France entered 1914 with five Armies made up of a total of 21 regional corps. Each corps had two 16,000 men divisions. Most divisions in the French Army at the time were considered triangular, in other words made up of three 3000-men regiments, with each regiment containing three battalions of about 1000 men.[27] And ideally, each battalion contained four companies of soldiers. At first, the army was comprised of mostly infantrymen, but by 1918 only about 40 percent of France's soldiers were artillerymen, with increasing percentages dedicated to special new equipment, such as the airplane, machine gun, armored car, and tank. [28]

As in most army units today, the company was the level where most soldiers interacted, the lowest common denominator. At full strength, each French infantry company numbered 250 men, most of them riflemen, including three officers: a captain and three lieutenants. The company was divided into four sections, much like modern units divide into platoons, and each section had four squads. Starting in 1915, however, as casualties and the availability of draft-able citizens

---

27   "Organization of an Infantry Company," http://www.151ril.com/content/history/french-army/6

28   "French Army and the First World War," http://spartacus-educational.com/FWWfrenchA.htm

decreased the pool of men from which the French army could draw, the company's theoretical maximum strength was reduced to 215 men. By the end of the war, the number had dropped further to 200 men. [29] As today, company borders are a bit fluid and soldiers might move around between companies in a regiment.

In 1914, the French draft and the induction center where Arthur and his companions were screened had become much more equitable than in times past. In the past, when exceptions were available to heads of households, for example, and those who could pay to have someone else take their place. With changes to France's draft rules in 1907 and the need for an exponential ramp up of men fit for duty in 1914, most deferrals for military service were granted only for medical reasons. Of his traveling companions, Army officials deferred Gustave Delneufcourt, who left to work in Trelissac in south-central France, and Fernand Mesquelier, who then went to Paris. Arthur's friends Deschamps, Bonnart, Fidias, Deltombe, and Lilert were accepted and sent to other military units and Arthur does not refer to them again. Likeable, even-tempered, and never the loner, Arthur quickly cultivated new friendships from passing acquaintances and met other men from Roubaix in the regiment.

For training, Arthur was assigned to the 84th Infantry Regiment in the First Army's 1st Division – Lille, 2nd Infantry Brigade de Cambrai, 84th Infantry Regiment from Avesnes. His brother Louis-Henry Jr, two years older, would have already been in his second year of compulsory military service. Arthur was assigned to the same division as his brother, but Louis-Henri was attached to the division's officer principal staff as part of the "corps d'etat major." Then, in mid-December Louis-Henri was reassigned to the 9th Battalion of Chasseurs de Pied.

The 9th Battalion of Chasseurs de Pieds was as part of

29   "Organization of an Infantry Company," http://www.151ril.com/content/history/french-army/9

a rapid-deployment unit supporting the infantry. "Chasseur" is a French term for "hunter," and Chasseurs de Pied and Chasseurs de Cheval were designations for rapidly-deployable light infantry and cavalry units, respectively. But French light army units of 1914 weren't the iconic lance-carrying, charge-in-a-straight line infantry and cavalry of Napoleon's time. These were machine gun-wielding, highly mobile units, considered among the best troops in the French Army at the time. [30] Think WWI's version of today's Special Forces, shock troops, snipers, and scouts, all teamed together.

Arthur's brother Louis-Henri plays prominently in Arthur's war diary. Louis-Henri, or simply Henri, had married Madeline, who traveled with Henri's and Arthur's parents to Holland shortly after Arthur left to enlist. Later entries in the diary indicate that Louis-Henri was wounded and eventually settled in Paris, where Madeline joined him and Arthur visited often. Statistically, Louis-Henri's wounds were likely from shrapnel, either from an artillery-launched shell, mortar or grenade. Such injuries accounted for an estimated 60 percent of the war's military fatalities. [31]

While it's possible Henri might have been more comfortable with a machine gun, his younger brother Arthur in 1914 would have been issued the standard equipment and an infantryman's uniform once he passed the board and was certified as combat able. That uniform included a woolen greatcoat, called the "gris de fer bleute," or bluish iron gray; brilliant red "madder" wool trousers; black leather, ankle-high, lace-up boots; a pin-striped flannel cotton shirt; pin-striped cotton underwear; white cotton suspenders; two pair of white wool socks; and a madder wool kepi, or what today might be called a legionnaire's hat, with its signature black leather visor

---

30   *Verdun: The Lost History of the Most Important Battle of World War I, John Mosier, Penguin Press, 2014, pg. 136*

31   *"The Shock of War," Caroline Alexander, Smithsonian Magazine On-line, September 2010, https://www.smithsonianmag.com/history/the-shock-of-war-55376701/*

and regimental patch sewn onto the front of the cap. [32]

Each soldier was also issued their unique "plaque d'Identite," or ID plaque, suspended from a black shoelace or leather strap, which they were required to always wear around the neck to identify their body should they be killed on the battlefield. [33]

32   "Uniform and Equipment of 1914," http://151ril.com/content/gear/1914

33   ibid

Chapter Two: Training

"*I would have liked to go with him but my brother thought that it was not my turn yet to go to the front. He makes me stay. I am alone without my brother or friends until January 28th when my unit is sent back to St-Agnan. There we resupply and prepare our departure for the front. Thankfully, I receive the first letter from my dear parents, post-marked from Holland. I open it and cannot stop myself from crying when I recognize Madeleine's writing.*

"*On January 30th we leave for St-Yriex where we meet with the frontline supply depot and are put up in a school for the night. The next day I am assigned to kitchen duty as a butcher. This I can do; I'm well and happy. The Corporal in my regiment, who has been really good to me, takes me with him to pick up food and kitchen supplies in preparation for field training. On February 4th we begin to pack up for departure and on the 6th we leave by train from St-Yriex. We go as far as Tuperly near Chalous, where we get off in the middle of the night. From the station, we can see the flares far in the distance. After we leave the station, things get much tougher. We walk from 2 o'clock in the morning until 9 o'clock, when we arrive at St-Remi-S-Busy.*

"*I am assigned to cook for my squad and soon afterwards I am cooking for the General Officer's kitchen. We go to the firing ranges at Chalous and upon our return, our squad is dispersed. I am assigned to stay with the leadership and the division in Drvareille. We embark in a convoy of cars to Dourmartin Lettre, where I continue to be a cook and butcher. Our division receives and sends reinforcements to units in battle but eventually the division, too, is dissolved. I am then sent to the 110th Infantry, which is camped at Vraux, 12 km from Chalous. After I report in, I am temporarily loaned to the 4th Division where I make a new friend, Plipo, who assists me with the cooking. We must get up early to prepare meals and go to bed late after cleaning the kitchen, but still we find time to visit the canteen and make friends.*

"*We stay in Vraux for eight days practicing maneuvers, then we march to Plivot, only to move on to Vertus because the Army does not have any barrack space for us. I arrive completely exhausted, my feet are bleeding, and still there are no bunks available. We are placed in private homes and the people who take us in are very good to us. I eat with them and sleep in a good bed. In fact, all things considered, we have a very good stay in Vertus, including attending nightly concerts. We pass in review in front of the General Staff and a few days later, on Sunday, we leave Vertus. We walk piou-piou to our next assignment, where we are treated by the towns people equally well. I am put to work again as a butcher for one day but we leave the next day for the Meuse, arriving in Fere that evening." [34]*

And so, Arthur became a pioupiou, or raw recruit, and soon the war would mold him into Arthur, the poilu, or hairy and scruffy veteran, one of "l'Ancien (the Ancient), a survivor. After the first year of the war, though, he would become just another of France's millions of "pitou," a term that became a respectful, general term for the French foot soldier.

Arthur in training must have been an Arthur amazed at the newness of his environment, a young man with a dawning awareness of the grave task his generation of citizen soldiers had inherited. Yet it wasn't in Arthur's nature to dwell on or become paralyzed by such philosophical thoughts. To serve was his duty; to serve well was a personal choice. A new conscript, he believed he could bring one very good skill into the fight: he knew how to cook. Very quickly he found himself in the kitchen as "le cuisinier," cooking for his comrades. Arthur mentions doing so almost casually, but it would have taken only a very short trial and error period to weed out pioupiou without such a skill. Those who knew how to use a pot and ladle would have found themselves reverently but enthusiastically escorted up to the stove, earning the title "le Cuistot," or in English, Cooky. And, just as cream rises, the best of the cooks found themselves serving the officers.

---

34   *By February 1915, La Fere would be 25 miles behind the German lines. ("Map of the Stabilized Front, http://www.emersonkent.com/map_archive/western_front_1915.htm)*

Cooking for a company of hungry men can be a thankless task. Before the cooking even starts, it requires vigilant sanitation, long-term planning, self-depreciation and humility, and creative substitution. Such responsibility might have weighed heavy on some men at a time when small infractions or infractions perceived by an almost omnipotent officer corps could bring harsh discipline but Arthur's mood remained light, he made friends, and mentioned that he even had some free time to spend in the canteen.

"Spending time in the canteen" for a French soldier in 1914, was similar to today's soldier deciding to drop into the on-post or on-base club. There were, however, some striking differences. It has been said that service in the French Army drives a soldier to drink but no man in the French Army drinks alone. [35] To do so, an act referred to as "faire Suisse," was considered not just antisocial, but mean-spirited. Not only was such a soldier thought to be hoarding his money, but the act of faire Suisse implied that the soldier detested spending off-duty time with his bunkmates, much less buy them a drink. This was considered a serious character flaw. After all, if a buddy would not share a franc in the canteen, would he share his last scrap of bread in the field, or his second-to-last bullet? To the French poilu, time in the canteen was an act of self-sacrifice and self-denial, a matter of honor. To drink alone was a broken trust that could result in a tossed bed or a blanket court-martial. [36]

A French military canteen was more than a bar: it was an inexpensive place to relax. A soldier could get a hard roll and a quality cup of coffee for three halfpence, a bottle of drinkable wine for fivepence, or good wine for a franc. Seldom was hard liquor or beer served, at least early in the war with only French patrons, and since a bottle was always shared, drunkenness was rarely a problem. It was, however, a place to hear or share a song,

---

35   *The French Army, pg. 51*

36   *A British term that refers to the group act of wrapping a fellow soldier in his own bedding, and with comrades holding onto four corners and sides of the sheet, repeatedly tossing the victim towards the ceiling.*

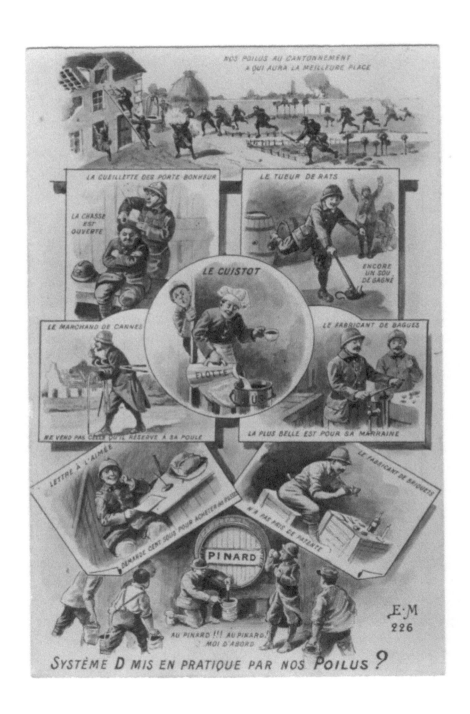

gather with friends who came from the same department, meet new ones from other departments, compare notes, and discuss events. Every canteen had a barber who shaved for free and each soldier was expected to see him at least twice a week (and shave themselves the other five days.) [37]

Eventually, although the sentiment of camaraderie continued in other forms, the canteen became a social service only available in military camps. The French Army was quickly growing its ranks with young men from all over France and the demand for barracks, bunks and bedding could not keep up. From late 1914 until almost the end of the war, soldiers could and often would find that they had been assigned to sleep with a local family and eat "on the economy" in a local tavern.

Consider the civilians' point of view during a brutal and destructive invasion. Their loyalties lie unquestionably with the defending army and they have complete sympathy for the plight of the common soldier with whom they now come into intimate and personal contact, on the streets, in the shops and cafes, and in their very homes at night. Yet, in the back of their minds must creep notions of what failure or defeat could look like in their future: eviction, or at the very least beds occupied by enemy soldiers; forced labor; pillaged food and fuel; and savings and currency that in a day become worthless.

Throughout recorded time, offensive and defensive military battles have erupted along the borders of two or more dissimilar cultures and there is no reason to believe such conflicts will ever cease in the future. Yet in the United States' modern history, its citizens have no collective experience that parallels the in-situ, defensive wars Europeans fought in the 18th, 19th, and 20th centuries. The closest analogue would be the Civil War more than 150 years ago.

---

37   *The French Army, pg. 55*

(Previous page) "Systems put into practice by our soldiers?," French humorous post card, illustrator unknown, addressed to "My dear little girl," October 5, 1917, but never mailed. Note that the cook is central to everything in the illustration.

Imagine a scenario today where a world power simultaneously invades Nome, Anchorage, and the Kenai Peninsula to control Alaska's vast oil and natural gas reserves. Or after heavy bombardment to soften resistance, an invading fleet docks in Baltimore, MD, or Oakland, CA, unloading hundreds of thousands of troops intent on marching into and capturing a prominent seat of government, and thus neutralize Washington's or California's international competition and influence.

Now imagine wanting, no, being required, to board American soldiers, young men and women, overnight, possibly every night, for years as your defending force fights back an invading one. Thousands of able-bodied and of-age youths – perhaps a spouse or your children – may be boarded in a house just like yours defending a town someplace else in the country. If you are deferred because you serve as the head of the household, perhaps you work a full-time job and then volunteer to prepare meals for the troops or refugees or you help in the hospitals. If you've been deferred from military service for health or other reasons, you may be working to support the home front as part of the civilian support corps. Everyone puts in a full day and then works some more, but to one degree or another, everything and everyone supports the country's defense.

In the evenings, people do what they can to divert their minds from the darkening uncertainty of tomorrow's news. Maybe they go to movies together, play team video games, or gather to dance and karaoke, but whatever occupies them in the evening, they do in groups. The activity is secondary to the need for social reinforcement. In the weeks after the terrorist attack in New York City in September, 2001, many Broadway theaters continued their afternoon and evening stage productions, sometimes even giving away tickets for free, not because there was a great demand, but to preserve a sense of "normal" and fight back a fear that the future would hold a new normal, one that would be alien, unpleasant, and irreversible.

At night, defending troops in our imaginary scenario would retire, some to assigned barracks that their units have set up in schools or sports arenas, and when those facilities are full, into the guest and children's bedrooms in suburbs and city brownstone row houses.

And when the sun comes up, the battle resumes. If a civilian is lucky enough, the fight that day is in someone else's neighborhood. Urban fighting is brutal combat: intersections that have been the centers of communication and commerce for a hundred years can be reduced in seconds to a stack of loose bricks in a crater. As if a tornado skipped indiscriminately through town, some blocks would appear untouched – except for the loss of water and power -- while others might cease to exist, at least in any recognizable form. Those civilians who could leave early are refugees someplace else. Those civilians who decide to stay and are not buried in the crater come out into the open air shell-shocked but alive once the battle moves on.

This imaginary scene might describe the "front lines" of Santa Rose, Antioch, or Fairfield, California, or perhaps Canton, Glen Burnie, or Fairfield, Maryland, but in the reality of the first world war, for Arthur it describes the life of a civilian along the Western Front in the smaller towns like Vertus, twenty miles as the crow flies south of Reims, and La Fere, 35 miles northwest of Reims. It was for small towns like these in northern France, as much as iconic Paris, that Arthur was in training to protect.

Arthur was initially sent to the 84th regiment for training, but except for a short detail with the 4th Division -- apparently to learn to cook -- he was eventually assigned to the 110th, part of France's 2nd Division which at that time was defending the city of Verdun.

Chapter Three: Easter, 1915

"We drive all night and the next day and when night comes we get out of the cars and march to the Isle de Barrois. At night, we sleep in civilian beds and begin to really appreciate what the people in the Meuse are doing for us. We leave the Isle and go to St-André, a little country of about a hundred habitants. We could not have picked a worse place to stop, but we stay the night there and get back on the road the next day, heading for Verdun. It is a long trip but we arrive at Glorieux Faubourg, just east of Verdun, on Holy Friday. We cannot wait to get to the trenches! We are awakened on Saturday at 3 o'clock in the morning, and by 5:00 a.m. we are off to go set up and stage from the barracks in the old part of town. We wait in Reserve there until they need us to relieve the front lines. During the day, we watch lines of Boch prisoners march back from the battlefield. It has rained for the last four days and they are really tired and dirty. We spend Easter Sunday in the barracks and I am able to attend mass, held outside by Father Choquel, a chaplain of the 110th. It is pouring rain again, but still we go to training Sunday afternoon. On Monday we rest, but we are told to be ready to leave on Tuesday. We stand ready in our quarters all day but we are not called up that night. Around 9 in the morning the next day, however, we move out, every step bringing us closer and closer into the line of fire."

Arthur, having "passed in review" and graduated from training, traveled by car and by foot with his regiment across north central France to Verdun. This is ten months before the beginning of the infamous and lengthy Battle of Verdun. The front at this point wrapped around the northern underground forts that circled the city's now venerable, walled fortress. Arthur's unit arrived at Fort Souville, a training camp across the Meuse River east of Verdun. At that point in the war, Fort Souville was about 10 km south of the front lines, probably close enough for residents to hear shells exploding and see the flash of German cannons off in the distance at night.

It is worth noting that up to this point in his journal, Arthur did not directly reference the enemy. Now, and from this point forward, he refers to the "Boch." [38] The term Boch or Boche, then a pejorative term but now more-or-less neutral slang, was a shortened version of the French word "alboche," a word derivative in French for German, or "Allemand," and a pun on the French word for a head of cabbage, or "cabochon," itself a derisive term meaning a thick-headed, disagreeable and troublesome person. [39] Arthur's use of the term presumably is an indication of his indoctrination into the infantry, his mind beginning to harden against an enemy he would soon face across the trenches.

It's impossible to fully appreciate the drive and sense of duty that young French males like Arthur felt about enlisting. It wasn't just that a German Army had invaded their country to take away regions of rightfully French soil or that the smoke on the horizon from the billowing cannons and their targets proved the inevitability of a fight. It wasn't just that these men felt they had to protect their families, wives, or livelyhoods. In 1914 France, the concept of the citizen soldier was cultural: service to France was simply an unquestionable duty.

At the risk of a boring history lesson, it's important to understand that from 1872 until the turn of the 20th century, the institution that was the French Army was the pride of France. Going back to Napoleonic times, the mystique of the French soldier, at least in the minds of the French, was one with the concept of national strength, honor, truth, and duty. In 1872, it became mandatory in France for every able French male citizen once he reached his 20th birthday, to give his country five years of active

---

38   Sometimes also found spelled as "Bosch" or "Bosche."

39   "Current History," New York Times Magazine, April-September, 1916

military service, five years in the defensive Territorial army, and six additional years in the Reserves.

Subsequently, changes in French laws in 1889 and again in 1905 dropped a French citizen's military service commitment to two years while eliminating exemptions for some males (family bread winners, for example, or those wealthy enough to buy out their term). The effect on French support for its military was dramatic: the burden of mandatory service was softened; voluntarism became more equitable between classes; and more men and their families shared or were exposed to the citizen soldier experience.

As a result, by 1910, virtually an entire country supported the idea of citizenship responsibility for military service. [40] Every man between the ages of 20 and 45 who was physically capable was a soldier, period. And every family had a soldier serving someplace. Each year, communities compiled a list of its eligible men. The "conseil de revision cantonale," a draft board of sorts, would revisit the list, and anyone once rejected was put back into examination. Mental and physical health were considerations, to be sure, and males shorter than 5' and one-half inches tall required a written waiver.

France in the first decade or so of the 20th century, however, was a country of growing national concerns. The British to the west and especially neighboring Germany to the east were formidable world powers. France had economic interests, and thus vulnerabilities, in their overseas colonies. To protect these colonies, Colonial governments required an additional 60,000 men. So, to address this shortfall, by 1914 the citizen solder in France was expected to give not 20 years but 25 years of service, and the mix had changed. French law now required of every able-bodied male to provide two or three years on active duty, augmented by an additional eleven in the

---

40   *"The French Army," by Ex-trooper, pg. 11*

Reserve, including periods of months of active Army training. The remaining service commitment was spent in the Territorial Army, after which a citizen was exempt from further military obligation.

Despite such numbers of citizens in uniform, France's careerist military looked on the use of reservists and non-career soldiers, especially in front-line units, with distain and distrust. [41] They saw the "citizen soldier" as unfit for the furious offensive operations dictated in new military doctrine. According to the prevailing attitude, Reservists would have neither the zeal nor strength to fight with glory and honor in bayonet combat. Besides, they argued, Reservists would never get that chance: any war was sure to be bloody but short, won by trained regular troops attacking always and everywhere. [42]

But the reality of the situation that the French Army was to face in WWI, especially during the very intense and prolonged battles to come, was that no soldier, career or reservist, could endure more than two weeks in the trenches. For example, the average period "in the line" (of fire) for French units at Verdun was eight days, not only due to the battle tempo but also to battlefield conditions. Winters and summers could be brutally cold and hellishly hot, and always wet. Allied commanders developed a complex troop rotation they called "the noria," North African slang for a shuttle system, [43] such as was used along caravan trails. Fresh or refreshed units would be held in reserve and called into duty like a chain or rope rotating around a well pulley, up into the light, then back down into the dark. British infantrymen typically spent one week during any given month fighting in the

41   *"No Other Law: the French Army and the Doctrine of the Offensive," Charles W. Anders, Jr., RAND Corporation, 1987, page 10*

42   *ibid*

43   *The Great War and the Shaping of the 20th Century, Jay Winter and Blaine Baggett, Penguin Books USA, NY NY, 1996, pg. 131*

line; one week as a stevedore, muleteer, or in some other support role; one week in reserve ready to deploy; and the fourth in training, on leave, or attending to other duties. [44]

That's not to say the typical French foot soldier became a specialist, at least not as modern soldiers know the term. Many never lived that long, but besides that, the nature, rotations, and pace of war required soldiers have a little knowledge in every discipline. In the same week, sometimes in the same day, a bottom-ranking pitou (also called "le Fantabosse, foot soldier," or "le lignard," lineman) might be ordered to serve as "l'eclaireur" (scout), "le courreur" (runner), "le canardeur" (sniper), "le brancardier" (stretcher-bearer), or to follow-up in the enemy trench as "le zigouilleur," a term politely referred to as trench cleaner, but more accurately meant "whacker," or killer.

It's no wonder that civilized men had to be rotated out of battle every few weeks.

---

44   *The Great War and the Shaping of the 20th Century, jay winter and Blaine Baggett, Penguin Books USA, NY, NY, 1996, pg. 132*

Chapter Four:
The battlefield at last

"We leave the barracks in Souville and march on until 4 o'clock in the afternoon, stopping in a clearing near the Rozeliers' fort to eat soup before we get back on our way. We are supposed to sleep at Sommes-Dieu but there is no room for us so we march on a little bit longer, already very tired. We find some quarters at Villers-en-Argonne, but like everywhere else in the Meuse, we are very badly settled. Around 10:00 at night, we receive orders to leave immediately to relieve a regiment at the Éfarges but since we are all very tired, the colonel answers that he cannot leave and our departure is postponed until the next day.

"In the morning we leave Villers-sur-Meuse and march towards the Éfarges village, crossing through some woods along the edge of Verdun. We get to the first communication trenches around 7:00 at night. Because we have been behind the cavalry and are tired from having to walk in mud, we get to the trenches at 4:00 in the morning. It has taken us nine hours to make 3500 meters. The regiments that are standing down mix with us in passing and it is complete chaos."

It was late April, 1915, again, ten months before the opening salvos of the Battle of Verdun, but more significantly to Arthur, it was just weeks after the German Army had repulsed France's 12th Division advances on this same battlefield, with heavy losses. The struggles for control of Les Esparges and the Woevre Plain beyond it to the east leading up to April 1915 produced the longest French casualty rosters up to that point in the war. [45]

For Arthur's unit, this was a significant redeployment. Orders took them from the Souville trenches north of Verdun, south to Fort Rozelier just west of Haudiomont by lunch

---

45   *The Great War and the Shaping of the 20th Century, jay winter and Blaine Baggett, Penguin Books USA, NY NY, 1996, pg.. 138*

time. Presumably they skirted the southern edge of Verdun and headed thirty miles west, leaving the Meuse Region and entering the Marne to spend the night at the Villers-en-Argonne. It had been a long day, and just as they were settling in for the night, they received orders to all but retrace their steps east back to the Meuse River, which they did the next day. The soldiers arrived at the Villers-sur-Meuse in the afternoon, crossed the river and marched into the rear encampment by mid-evening. A short rest to regroup and to give the officers a moment to communicate with the battle staff, and the unit was sent off to relieve a regiment in the trenches along a ridge to the east of a small village on Verdun's southern flank, Les Esparges. The 1000-foot high ridge, also called Les Esparges, and its companion mesa, Combres, were strategically critical, providing an observation point across the Woevre Plain to the east. If the French were to attempt to retake the Woevre Plain to prevent a German advance on Verdun from below, they would need to control this ridge. [46]

It took Arthur's unit nine hours to cross just a little more than two miles to reach the regiment. By the time they got there, it was predawn and the soldiers they were to replace, near to panic from hours of waiting, were dangerously and probably carelessly joyful for the relief.

---

46   *Verdun: The Lost History of the Most Important Battle of World War I, John Mosier, Penguin Press, 2014, pg. 135*

PART THREE:
LES EPARGES, THE MARNE, VERDUN

Napoleon Bonaparte said, "Glory is fleeting, but obscurity is forever." World War I historians, military strategists, and popular media who have reported on the fighting along the Western Front have traditionally focused on the region's epic battles: Verdun, the Somme, Meuse, Ypres, etc. They date each conflict as between its opening artillery barrage and the noticeable silence left after the last shell has dropped. Without question, such conflicts deserve the attention, reflection, and scrutiny these students of war give them. In most cases, the terrible loss of life, atrocious application of modern technology, and the relatively few military gains and national goals achieved over so many years all but demands it. While the great battle receives its glorious attention, however, the lesser one becomes obscure and is almost forgotten.

General Bonaparte's quote appropriately applies to the soldiers who found themselves in the trenches along the Western Front just before or just after such battles. The same could be said of those whose luck it was to "stand the line" along uncontested ground or in times of quiet defense while fierce fighting went on elsewhere. To those men who survived the fiercest battle went the right to tell its story. Men who stood faithfully in quiet, ignored sections of the line or who served in one of the thankless but enabling jobs – laying railroad ties, cooking, shoeing mules – often earned little to brag about, only obscurity.

Such men are often the quiet ones after the war. Perhaps they feel survivor's guilt, having come through the experience at the expense of others who seemingly gave so much more. Perhaps they feel, unjustly so, that they somehow contributed less to winning than their comrades. Nothing could be farther from the truth: a soldier goes where he's told to go and performs his duty to the full measure of his physical and mental strength. He is a part of a larger strategy, a brick in the wall trusting that his generals and grand politicians will use brick and mortar wisely, not wastefully.

Perhaps Arthur survived the Great War because he was assigned duties and stations that averaged out to be quieter and safer than what other soldiers had been assigned. It's a fact that over the full course of the war, from October 1914 until he was released from duty in 1919, Arthur found himself in both the thick of battle and the quiet of its meantime, yet he survived while many of his fellow infantrymen did not. Perhaps it was his Catholic faith or his determination to do his duty for France. Perhaps it just wasn't his destiny to be counted as one of the war's casualties. Maybe it was only chance that neither machine gun bullet nor obus found him a target, or that neither chlorine gas nor cholera knocked him down.

Arthur entered his first battle at Les Eparges armed with his Frenchman's sense of duty and his luck. Weaving in and out of the fray, he would find himself defending the Line or standing up away from it, whichever he was called to do. For the next four years, he rotated through a cycle that appeared to have no end: fighting in the trenches, then standing ready in reserve; serving behind the lines, then recharging on permission, all choreographed so he could approach the line once again and repeat it.

Chapter One:
Arrival at the front

"The sun is rising and the Boch just saw us. They have started to launch shells on us. An obus explodes just over our heads, the first one that I have seen up close. I am close enough to have the breath knocked out of me when the third shell explodes. It kills a lieutenant from the 8th Company and hurts a captain and a few men. Then a little bit later it is the commandant who is hurt. The shelling splits us up and I get separated from my regiment but I rejoin them a little bit later. Now it is time to attack and we cross the infamous "ravine of death." It is covered with cadavers from days of fighting and they smell really bad. We take some ground and then are relieved for a while, my section placed in reserve. We start to dig ourselves individual holes that we cover with anything we can find, like artillery shell crates or pieces of damaged bracing. Boch spotter planes have been flying over us for almost an hour now, directing shelling from the rear. For a while the French are dominant, then it is the Boch. Our artillery shoots down a Tourb, and we all yell in excitement, but then almost immediately an obus comes in and hits a man from the 1915 training class. He is killed instantly. The planes having found our position, we are shelled again. An obus hurts a friend to my left pretty badly, then a little bit later explosions hurt two others. I see my time coming and more than once I pray for my life. After four days of suffering with barely anything to eat, we are forced to get water from the holes that the obus left since the village is too far away and too destroyed to go get water there."

Arthur refers to the obus, his generic term for an exploding artillery shell. "Obusier" simply means howitzer in French. This early in the war, late 1914 and early 1915, the German army was using their older 7.7 cm Feldkanone, or FK96s; the 15cm schwere Feldhaubitze, called the sFH-13; and the 42cm M-Great howitzer, nicknamed Big Bertha. [47]

---

47   *"German Empire Artillery of World War 1, https://www.militaryfactory.com/armor/ww1-german-artillery.asp*

A young American Red Cross volunteer was to write in 1916: "There was a sound like the roar of an express train, coming nearer at tremendous speed with a loud singing, wailing noise." He was describing an incoming artillery round. "It kept coming and coming and I wondered when it would ever burst. Then, when it seemed right on top of us, it did, with a shattering crash that made the earth tremble. It was terrible. The concussion felt like a blow in the face, the stomach and all over; it was like being struck unexpectedly by a huge wave in the ocean." [48]

The term for being exposed to such a blast was "being blown up." [49] Arthur, in an almost off-handed way, dismissed

364. La Grande Guerre 1914-15 — Campement d'artilleurs en WOËVRE
In Woëvre villages constructed by french soldiers   • Phot-Express •

---

48   "The Shock of War," Caroline Alexander, Smithsonian Magazine On-line, September 2010, https://www.smithsonianmag.com/history/the-shock-of-war-55376701/

49   ibid

(Above)   French postcard, "Artillery encampment in the Woevre" mailed to Paris, 4/4/15. Image and printing by Photo-Express.

as nearly irrelevant any harm from the first concussive blast of the obus that he received. After all, it didn't appear to do him any harm and others in the trenches were worse for wear than he. True enough, but in the course of the war, he was to "be blown up" tens, if not hundreds of times.

If repeated tackles and body blocks can cause head trauma in professional football players, imagine an NFL football player repeatedly blown back by exploding offensive linesmen. Shells did not fall randomly, one and done. Preceded by an increasingly shriller scream as they descended, each shell was dropped in a bombardment pattern with ever more deadly accuracy thanks to spotters perched in the highest ridge tops and in aircraft overhead. In either case – on a hill top or up in the sky – control of higher ground won or lost battles. The same is true today.

This early in the war, planes like the Austrian Taube were mostly used for reconnaissance. Eventually, airmen might carry hand-dropped bombs or surveillance cameras, but more likely over Arthur's trenches at Les Esparges, aviators used gestures and shouting, signal pennants, or wing wags to mark enemy-filled trenches. More on the aircraft in later chapters, but it is sufficient to say that in 1915 use of the airplane over the battlefield was evolving. For example, by late 1916, wireless radio technology had evolved to the point where radio telephones could be used in British cockpits, and shortly after that came the built-in helmet microphone and earphone to block out background noises. [50] With the advancement of technology came ever-evolving applications, new tactics, and eventually strategic uses for the airplane in battle.

Whether used for recon or for bombing runs, the airplane had one nemesis, and no, it wasn't the artillery shell. It was rain, the infantryman's best and worst friend. In April

---

50   "Ten Inventions that owe their success to WWI," Stephen Evans, BBC News (http://www.bbc. com/news/magazine-26935867)

and May, the Woevre Valley would have been waterlogged. In fact, "Woevre" comes from a word that means wet. [51] It was the rainy season, and although Arthur didn't describe the weather much when he wrote of his first trench encounter, he mentioned that the craters filled with water, presumably either as seep from past rains or from the light drizzles and mist that are an almost daily occurrences west of Verdun during that time of year. Rain, and its sidekick, mud, made the infantryman's life a dark and slow-motion nightmare. Clothes, boots, even food, were never dry. Mud built up on boots and wagon wheels. But rain and fog also helped keep fire from spreading in the trenches. It provided cover when soldiers topped the "ravine of death," filled shell holes with water to drink, and swatted back the bothersome Taube flying aircraft, grounded as useless when visibility was poor.

---

51   *Verdun, The Lost History of the Most Important Battle of World War I, John Mosier, Penguin Books, 2014, pg. 142*

Chapter Two: Les Eparges

"Around the night of the 4th day we learn that reinforcements are coming. We cannot believe it until we are told to get our packs ready and to leave and regroup in the Éparge village. By 3:00 in the morning everyone has assembled and we leave silently. The division has lost a lot of good men; we have barely 60 left. We stay at Montair-le-grand hotel where, after having taken a shower (we are literally covered with mud), we reassemble and pass-in-review before General Lery and his staff. We leave for a quiet village where at the top of a mountain, I visit the mass grave of 150 French soldiers and as many Germans. It is peaceful there and we stay five days recovering. Eventually, we leave by foot for Willers-en-Argonne, then travel in cars for Coussans-sous-Bois. After three days in Coussans-sous-Bois, we are required to leave to reinforce the 8th in the Ailly Wood, who have taken quite a beating. We leave at 8 o'clock in the evening, our spirits improved somewhat, the white wine of Coussans-sous-Bois giving us the strength to approach the front yet again. But when we get there, everything is completely chaotic. Nobody knows where the Boch are, and we learn that a whole battalion of the 8th has been taken prisoner. Soon afterwards, we leave the Meerain for the Commanderie where we receive the order to hold our ground at any cost. Fortunately, it is night and since the Boch cannot see us from upon their perches overlooking the Meuse, they miss their chance to have at us.

"Around 2:00 in the morning we receive orders to return to Coussans and by 5:00 a.m. we are back in our quarters there. After a few days, we travel by cars to Dieu. On the way, we are seen by an enemy flying division. We figure out immediately that they now know our position and strength. We pass the night in Dieu, and the next afternoon while it is pouring rain, we sneak back to the lines at Mouilly, holding our position in the big trench at Calorine. Our assigned guides, however, barely know where we are, so we are forced to stay in the same spot for two hours while they get their bearings. Eventually, they come back to get us. We take the point and the rest of the soldiers move to the rear as the 12th Division stands down in reserve.

"In the morning a group of Bavarians lead a Boch attack and we are sent to reinforce a breach in one of the first line trenches, even though the trenches are already full of people. The Boch know we are coming and open an attack with a crossfire. We arrive at the front trench, but we have suffered some casualties, including our Lieutenant who had his thumb cut off by a bullet. At 11:00 in the evening, the Boch attack starts in earnest and the firing lasts all night. They cannot dislodge us but during the night, we burn more than 100,000 cartridges defending our position. The next evening, we make a push on the right flank, make some headway, and wait there for reinforcements. We are all tired: it has been eight days and we have barely slept."

On April 5th, France attempted an offensive at Les Eparges, a 346-meter mesa to the southeast of Verdun. Ultimately, it was not successful, with France's 1st Army losing more than 2,700 officers and 15,500 soldiers. As part of the battle, the Germans had established a salient [52] at Bois d'Ailly, or the Ailly Woods, strategically important for its view overlooking Saint-Mihiel and the Meuse River. The French had attacked it during the first week of April, but by the time Easter has passed, the German Army had abandoned about 700 meters of trenches that they could not or desired not to defend. [53] The French moved in to occupy the ground but the Germans countered and by the end of April had overrun a four-kilometer span of French holdings, including several pieces of large artillery. German units attacked again on May 4th. In short, the battle to capture Les Eparges was a gruesome defeat for the French, who lost an estimated 123,000 soldiers.

---

52   *A salient, or projection in a battle line, can be a tactically delicate thing, presenting both opportunity and risk, depending on what the holder intends to do next. Although it can serve to divide an enemy, it also exposes two flanks, the right and left sides of the salient.*

53   *Verdun, The Lost History of the Most Important Battle of World War I, John Mosier, Penguin Books, 2014, pg. 143*

France's 8th Infantry Division took the brunt of the fighting to protect Verdun and it was Arthur's division's task to provide some relief. The 8th had been created in the French 4th Army at the beginning of the war as part of the garrison at the Verdun Fortress, but as action with the Germans intensified, forcing France to reorganize its defensive strategy, the 8th was subordinated to the French 3rd Army.

Arthur 's 110th Regiment was assigned to France's 2nd Division, which fought in the first Battle for the Woevre from April 5 until the middle of May. [54] Arthur's unit was rotated out and back into battle over the course of several weeks, but by early May, it became clear that the French offensive to take the bluffs overlooking the Woevre Valley was unsuccessful. Not necessarily a rout but a defeat none-the-less, French units fighting on the mesa of Les Eparges were ordered to retreat, regroup, and await further instructions.

54   Second Infantry Division, France," https://fr.wikipedia.org/wiki/2e_division_d%27infanterie_(France)

Chapter Three:
May to November, 1915

"Eventually, we are reinforced by the 126th Infantry and settle at Sommedieue. After three good nights there, we receive orders to leave the Meuse department and proceed west to the Marne. We embark for Saint-Remy-sur-Bussy, heading back towards Vertus, where we arrive on Sunday morning. I am temporarily assigned to an unloading team but I soon return to my division at Damerie, a nice little country on the bank of the Marne River. The habitants are very good to us and help us forget (a little) about our defeat further upriver. After four days of rest, we travel by cars north towards Vantelay. From the road we can see Reims off in the distance, recognizing the city by its famous cathedral. It does not seem damaged. We spend the evening in Vantelay and when night comes we head out for the Miette Wood located in front of Poutaverté on the Aisne. My division is to be held in reserve so we dig shelters along a stream, working quickly to settle in. After three days, on May 20, I go to a meeting at the division's command post in the brigade at the 8th Infantry. I meet up with Marcel Lucoulle who is in the same division, and together we are sent to Brassecourt as instructors. After 15 days of teaching, I stay in Vantelay to serve as a muleteer. It is 15 calm and quiet days.

"On June 13th I'm called to cook for the officers and by the 20th I am back in the woods with my regiment, where I am assigned care of the ordinary. A little while later, I am also given responsibility for the field-kitchen at Curie-les-Chaudardre, which serves Colonel Lenoir. Our division stays in the area until August 22, when we are reinforced by the 33th, allowing us to leave to join with Colonel Lenoir at Curie-les-Chaudardres. We are only there a short while, then we move on to Jugencourt, then to Cormicy. The division is called to the front lines at

Sapigneul. [55] I spend eight days in charge of the line kitchen and pass the Toussaint at Courmicy."

With the last battles to control Les Eparges plateau over, at least for a while, Arthur's regiment was relieved from the line and pulled north several miles closer to Verdun into less contested territory. They were still on the east bank of the Meuse River, poised to be recalled quickly into battle if the Germans had pushed their victory and reengaged. With the battle all but over, Arthur's division was sent westwards from the Meuse River, across the Marne River at Damery, 60 miles downriver to the west, ending up about 16 miles south of Reims. From there, his division skirted Reims to take up a position across the Ainse River on the border between the Marne and Ainse departments. While his unit began to establish themselves there, Arthur was sent to help train new recruits back in Ventalay, just over the Ainse and Marne department line. After a couple of weeks of this, Arthur didn't immediately return to his unit. Instead, he stays to serve as a muleteer transporting supplies and as a cook, again in the general officer mess.

At this point, it is worth adding a little background about French officer and soldier rank, chain-of-command, and unit structure. Arthur mentions both officer and rank enlisted casualties in his writings, as if they were serving side-by-side in the trenches. They were.

Military chain of command and the ratio of officers to soldier in the French Army was, at least at the start of Arthur's Great War, very rigid. A soldier's colonel headed the regiment. With the help of his senior staff, the "Conseil d'Administration, he was responsible for the unit's every need: discipline, sanitation,

---

55   *Unfortunately, Sapigneul was strategically placed overlooking the Ainse River and a canal that connected the Ainse to the Marne. Once a pastoral hamlet of farms and a small church, Sapigneul was completely destroyed two years later and was never rebuilt. Deemed by authorities as still too dangerous and contaminated to dig in, it now sits in a "red zone," an area cordoned off against any human habitation, visitation, or development.*

security, promotions, logistics, etc. His second-in-command was the lieutenant colonel, who was responsible for such duties as the conduct of the unit's officers and writing reports. Below that, each regiment had two majors who commanded the service squadrons, responsible for payroll, purchasing and tracking supplies, military police matters, and running the all-important mess hall and canteen.

Reporting to the majors in each regiment were a number of captains who managed the day-to-day operations for not only duties of the line – executing battlefield tactics and orders – but also such tasks as paymaster or training. Among the captains in each squadron would be a Capitaine Commandant and a junior, or second, capitaine, with the senior captain in charge of unit military education, discipline, troop pay, and horses (in cavalry units) and the junior captain responsible for the canteen, daily roll calls, and guard duties.

When at full strength, each squadron would have also included four lieutenants, each responsible for a peloton, or platoon; two doctors and/or two horse veterinarians; a number of adjutants (roughly equal to the British rank of warrant officer), sergeants, and corporals. Serving the senior captain, the highest-ranking non-commissioned officer in a squadron was the sergeant-major. [56]

It was considered unusual for a foot soldier to see, much less come in contact with, a general officer in a twelve-month period, so Arthur's cooking for the general and his staff is an important detail.

June 13, 1915 marked a turning point for Arthur. Up to this point, he had distinguished himself as a veteran in the trenches. He had served as a muleteer and a strongback unloading supply wagons. Several months before, though, Arthur had been assigned to cook for his unit and was soon cooking for the General

---

56   *"The French Army from Within," by "Ex-trooper," published by George H. Doran Company, 1914, pg. 27-33*

152. Guerre 1914-15. — LE BOURGET. Soldats faisant la soupe.   " Col. Pays de France"

French postcard, "Soldiers making soup," WWI, Le Bourget (ten miles northeast of Paris) circa 1914-1915

Officer's mess. Now in the field, he was called on once again to cook and this time his skills were formally recognized and he was assigned responsibility for the ordinary [57] and eventually a field kitchen. While this did not pull him off of the front lines, it likely reduced his exposure somewhat to live fire in future trench fighting and possibly helped him dodge the one bullet or obus explosion that would have changed the outcome of his story.

      Shells from the long cannons on both sides, what Arthur describes as the obus, took the battle at the front to well behind the first line trenches. Even the second line trenches and further back, the command and communication camps, were not immune to artillery fire. In Arthur's line of work, the constant shelling made field kitchens impractical. The French invented canning early in the 1800s and French soldiers received "iron rations" before approaching the Front, but with so many men in battle, canned

---

57   *Military for "mess hall," which is military for "cafeteria"*

foods were in short supply. Troops subsisted instead on fresh bread, fruit, sausages, and a cheap white wine, called "pinard." [58] Warm meals in the trenches were a rarity and generally limited to soup or stew, or perhaps hot coffee. [59]

Eventually in 1915, the French introduced a portable field kitchen of sorts, with meals prepared behind the lines and brought to soldiers in the trenches in large catering tins packed in bulky backpack-like racks carried by "l'homme-soupe," or soup men. In the French Army, the duty of soup man was considered more dangerous than line infantryman, requiring the soldier assigned to the detail to cross land in the scope of enemy machine guns and artillery encumbered with a large and heavy load. The mud made walking in such conditions extremely difficult and if the shooting started, the bulky load made it impossible to run or hide. [60]

Curiously, in contrast, British soldiers considered being a cook a much safer profession than infantryman; and by necessity, occasionally every soldier eventually would draw trench food delivery duties, called "Death by Dixie." While there were no Army catering corps in the modern concept of field mess halls and professional staff, and although in the trenches soldiers still fended for themselves, British troops were typically provided commercial-quality "tinned" meats, fish, hash, beans, stews, even milk. Behind the front lines and in reserve units, the British provided a cook for every 100 men. [61]

That's not to say large French and British mess halls didn't

---

58   *A French soldier after the war described pinard as a wine worthy of running in a car radiator, which can make the fluid almost drinkable.*

59   *"Ratatouille Froid: French Army Rations in WWI, http://17thdivision.tripod.com/ rationsoftheageofempire/id16.html*

60   *ibid*

61   *"The Battle to Feed Tommy," Adrian Lee, Daily Express, August 23, 2014, https://www. express.co.uk/news/world-war-1/502452/The-Battle-to-feed-Tommy-The-diet-of-a-WW1-soldier*

exist. They did, but mainly at headquarters and rear echelon facilities, near hospitals, training camps, and major railheads far from enemy lines.

With the exception of a short period when he served as a trainer, from May until the Feast of Toussaint, 1916 (All Saints Day, November 1), Arthur bounced around and across the Ainse River and canal. His unit dug in on the north side in Pontaverte and Arthur managed their meals, but since he was also responsible for the officer's field kitchen, presumably he split his time traveling to Curie-les-Chaudardre, a few miles to the west. Eventually, his division consolidated at Curie-les-Chaudardre, but they soon moved to Jugencourt, then to Cormicy, and the front-line trenches of Sapigneul.

Chapter Four:
Forced March

"This evening we buried four of our friends that an obus killed all at once, among them one from Roubaix, Lecaillon. We are reinforcements for the front trenches and wait back in Miette to be called to the line. On November 29, I go on a leave of absence. I come back on December 7, to Jouchery, where I find my division at the Butte de l'Edgnurd, behind Caronne. I sleep with the 4th section in the Bois de Bounnarous then we all meet at the Butte. I cook for the men working to reinforce our "caves" in the trenches. Ours shelters are nicer than most since we are assigned to the Division General's staff. We spend Christmas Eve dinner with the cooks of the 110th and go back to our shelters at 2:00 in the morning. A week later we throw a New Year's party but we are disturbed by the Boch, who attack us. At the beginning of the year we converge in the Stuan Wood. I still cook. My section is assigned to leave for St-Briée near Reims to instruct at the small depot there. We stay 15 days quartered in a cotton-mill and are treated very well. I serve as a muleteer for a few days. When the instruction ends, we get back to the division, which has just arrived from Rosnay. While we were away there was a complete switch of officers and staff. We leave from Rosnay to go set up our bunks in Lagery under pouring rain that does not stop until we arrive in our quarters. Soaking wet, I change my clothes and go to bed right away.

"The next evening, we are told to prepare to be ready for any kind of situation and the day after that we indeed leave in forced march up to a place near Epernay. We have walked 31 km and arrive exhausted. The next day at 10 o'clock, we embark for Vano-le-Chatel and arrive well before the dinner hour hoping for a hot meal, or at least some soup but the kitchens never come. We go the whole day without rations. The countryside has little to offer us and the habitants have little for themselves. We wait in Vano-le-Chatel for three days without knowing where along the front lines we will be sent to intervene. Some say it is going to be at Reims; others at Verdun. We walk for a while, we sleep at Noirlieu for

74.

one night, and then the whole regiment loads into a convoy of cars and heads back to Verdun. We travel more than a 100km by car and arrive in the outskirts of Verdun where we get off at Glorieux.

"It is February 26, 1916. It has been snowing since morning, it is very cold, and we now must carry all of our things on our backs."

During late Fall, 1915, Arthur's unit was still fighting on the Ainse River and canal. After suffering heavy losses on the front lines, they were relieved and recovered in reserve status a few miles southeast in Miette. By the time Arthur returned from a few days of personal leave, his unit had established itself south of Craonne. Almost 102 years earlier, Napoleon found himself fighting a combined Prussian and Russian army on these same hills and fields. Arthur division was placed in Craonne, just a few miles north of the Marne River, which marked the border between the Marne and Aisne departments. Their mission was to prevent German advances into Reims.

By Arthur's reports and tone, all was well in January 1916, if not peaceful, at least there was routine. He cooked, was detailed to train some new recruits, and even served as a muleteer for a while. Then, suddenly everything changed. A new staff took over and his unit was sent with little notice, provisions, or instruction by forced march. They redeployed on foot, not by car or truck, an indication that there was little time to make such arrangements. Arthur's unit traveled southeast, covering about sixty miles in three days, passing under Reims to Vanaut-le-Chatel. They had not been told why, but since they were marching ever eastwards, the speculation in the ranks was that they were heading back to Verdun. After another days' march, apparently their motorized transportation caught up with them and the unit covers 100 kilometers, arriving at the outskirts of Verdun on February 26, 1916, a week after the start of the German offensive to take the city.

Motorized transportation must have been a godsend

75.

after so much marching. Such a trek from the Somme region
to the Marne would not have been easy. For one thing, it was
January and winter snow, slush, or mud on small country roads
would have made the hike challenging. But throw a pack of
personal items on the back of each soldier and a haversack of
ammunition across their bodies and hips, and the march became
strenuous. British soldiers packed a mess tin, spare clothes,
wash kit, and a waterproof ground sheet in their pack, plus
a water bottle and a trenching tool, [62] but in addition to all
of that, the French infantryman also carried a camp stew pot,
a canvas bucket, and either a coffee grinder or a lantern. [63]
To add to their load, Arthur's unit and presumably the mule
or horse-drawn support carts, would have transported their
own battlefield material, including communications equipment,
portable kitchens, tents, and possibly mortars, barbed wire, and
more.

Historians peg February 21 as the official start of the
Battle of Verdun, and it was to last in a fever pitch until the
middle of December. Even today, it is considered by most
military historians as not only the longest battle of World War
1, but of any war. Arthur arrived a week into it.

---

62   From 'For King and Country' exhibit, Bankfield Museum, Halifax, England

63   "Uniform and Equipment, 1914," http://151ril.com/content/gear/1914

Chapter Five: Verdun,
February to March, 1916

"After getting out of the cars, we take the road to the Chevert station. The road seems especially long since we have everything on our backs, every one of us carrying 30kg of equipment, plus our personal gear. When we arrive at our assigned quarters, they are already full of troops, 85 of us in a place built for 40 men. It is not really a barracks, just a large hallway but we get some rest anyway and at 3:00 in the morning the officers wake us up to assemble outside in the terribly cold weather. The wind is fierce and it is freezing.

"Our combined unit walks up to Fleury still carrying all of our equipment on our backs. We arrive in Fleury and to our surprise we discover that the heavy artillery is leaving. We figure out what's going to happen. A little further on we come upon a squad of Chausser hidden behind the ridge cress. They have built a nest in the ground and are firing their machine-guns. I count more than 40 guns and I see that even in the freezing cold, our gunners are in undershirts firing away. We pass them and move across the part of Fleury that has not received any shelling yet. We can see signs in and around the village that we plan to be here awhile to defend Fleury: some field-kitchens, artillery boxes, and ambulances that belong to the regiment that we are reinforcing have been left for us. We head towards the ravine on the west side of the village, the Haudremont. We get in battle formation and wait for orders. Around 7:00 in the evening, a taube flies over and locates us. It makes some signals to the German artillery and that earns us a barrage of Boch heavy shells. We flank left since the 1st battalion already has a dozen men ready for combat on the right. We regroup in a small quarry and settle in. Around noon the next day, a big heavy shell falls approximately 50 meters from us and hurts one man. It is the first casualty of our division, a Boch 'Welcome to Verdun.'"

In January 1916, French airmen had detected a build-up of German offensive equipment and troops on the east bank of the Meuse River north of Verdun. A French intelligence officer confirmed those field reports on February 11. French commanders, preoccupied with plans for their own offensive, began to quickly regroup, pulling men and equipment from wherever they could. They would have had to reroute supply and logistics chains as well, to support these new movements and then compensate for such disruptions. [64]

Ten days later, on February 21, the German offensive for Verdun began. Today, thousands of hectares of landscape north and east of Verdun still bear the scars of ten months of continuous battle more than 100 years ago. Bomb craters and long-abandoned trenches pocket regrown forest and barren fields and signs mark the former locations of nine villages, never rebuilt. Fleury was one of those towns. In many of the ravines and fields to the north and east of Verdun, unexploded ordinance and arsenic-soaked soil are still so hazardous that "red zones" have been establish that prohibit construction or digging of any kind. [65]

Fort Douaumont, a major underground fortress about five miles north of Verdun, had fallen four days before. Fleury, or more properly Fleury-devant-Douaumont ("Fleury in front of Fort Douaumont"), lay between Fort Douaumont and the city. The local government had evacuated all of Fleury's 422 villagers to either Verdun and Bras-sur-Meuse on February 16. [66]

Arthur's unit set up in the Haudremont Ravine in Fleury just as the French were evacuating all of their heavy artillery. To the French infantrymen, this was not a good sign. Above all,

---

64   "Battle of Verdun," Britannica Encyclopedia Online, https://www.britannica.com/event/Battle-of-Verdun

65   "The Ghost Villages of Verdun," Vincent Kessler, Reuters, March 20, 2014 (http://blogs.reuters.com/photographers-blog/2014/03/20/the-ghost-villages-of-verdun/)

66   "Fleury-devant-Douaumont-Destroyed Villages of Verdun, Travel France Online, (https://www.travelfranceonline.com/fleury-devant-douaumont-destroyed-village-verdun-wwi/)

even above the lives of its men, the French Army would not risk having their artillery captured, and the soldiers knew that when the artillery retreated, a major offensive by the enemy was imminent.

Artillery was so valuable to the French that it is credited with having led to the development of the concept of camouflage (at least according to the French). In August 1914, two 6th Artillery Regiment Frenchmen, Lucien Victor Guirandd de Scevola and Louis Guingot, were the first to use branches and canvases painted in earth tones and textures to hid their guns. They also designed earth-colored coats for their gunners, which hid their strikingly-blue artillerymen's uniforms in the landscape. A year later, after several successful field experiments, the French Army established the first military Camouflage Section in Paris, made up of sculptors,

"The War, 1914-1915, The North Region, Adjusting artillery fire," French propaganda post card, published by Vise Paris, Number 270, unmailed.

metal workers, plasters, carpenters, mechanics, and painters (especially cubist artists, having learned to break down the image of an object into representational shapes). Initially applied to artillery, eventually the defensive technique of concealment and deception known as camouflage was applied to railroad equipment, trucks, boats and ships, and aircraft. [67]

---

67   *"Camouflage," Cecile Coutin, 1914-1918 Online International Encyclopedia of the First World War, https://encyclopedia.1914-1918-online.net/article/camouflage, October 2014.*

Chapter Six: Half rations

"For two days now we have been pinned down and have not been able to receive supplies or reinforcements. When we are down to our reserve food, we are given the order to eat at half rations. At 8:00 the second evening, I am assigned to make a run for cartridges in Fleury, which is now in flames. [68] The shells will not stop falling but we make it to town. In one of the few houses left standing, we actually find some bread casually stashed by the division that we are reinforcing. We take charge of the loaves and bring them back to the rest of the division waiting in the ravine, along with some jelly... and alcohol! At 10 o'clock the shelling has quieted, but while we are resting we receive the order to move back to the Haudremont ravine where we first set up camp. While on our way, the Boch will not stop shooting at us but they do not hurt anybody. We walk slowly and quietly in the dark to the ravine and around 4:00 in the morning, we finally reach it."

Units advance, hold, and retreat. Arthur reported that he and his fellow soldiers waited in an old rock quarry for two days before relief came and they could stand down.

At the beginning of the battle, February 21, France's front lines north and east of Verdun extended about five miles further out but by the time Arthur's unit arrived back at their station in Fleury's Haudremont Ravine, the village was nearly on the front lines and it was in flames. It is likely that some of the command staff and support soldiers had retreated to Verdun or the relative safety of nearby Fort Souville.

On March 5th, Arthur's unit probably was surprised when the Germans changed their strategy, literally taking a different approach. German forces turned and attacked on the

---

68   *Arthur refers to Fleury-devant-Douraumont, a small village about 2.5 miles northeast of Verdun. Eventually, most of Fleury-devant-Douraumont was obliterated under 90,000 tons of bombs in one day alone. (http://blogs.reuters.com/photographers-blog/2014/03/20/the-ghost-villages-of-verdun/)*

west bank of the Meuse, eventually taking Forges before being stopped in Morthomme on March 8. This new offensive likely took some pressure off of the French infantrymen fighting in the small villages and hamlets on the east bank, allowing the French some movement and their commanders an opportunity to bring in reinforcements and supplies. [69]

"Street picture from the destroyed Verdun," German propaganda post card, publisher Julius Berger. Mailed by German soldier, December 26, 1916.

---

69   *"The Battle of Verdun," Universal City Online, ng.verdun.fr/Universal-city/Verdun-and-World-War-I/The-Battle-of-Verdun*

Chapter Seven: No cover

"Up to now – at least today -- all is calm and we have not had but that one casualty. From time to time the Boch lob a few shells, but those do not cause much damage. But around 9:00 a.m. an airplane passes overhead, then two, then four, then six until twelve Boch planes have carefully pinpointed our position. It does not take long before the long guns know where we are. Up to this point we have not seen any French planes although if you believe the newspapers, our aviators are courageously flying everywhere. We are constantly moving around but at this point the regiment has taken up positions on the east slope of the Haudremont ravine where we quickly dig and reinforce our individual holes. For some, this will be their last home. Our sector is completely devoid of fortification, no buildings, no cover. On the contrary, we are completely exposed, with no opportunity to hide out of sight of enemy planes. We have arranged for a water convoy but it cannot make it past the Boch snipers who have the line-of-sight angle advantage from a position in a farm house opposite from us. The day before, that house was intact but now it is a pile of smoking ruins. It is a good thing none of us are badly wounded because with the Boch in complete control of the farm, it would be impossible to carry anyone to safety.

"At 10 a.m., the Colonel's PC and I are assigned to go to try to search the surrounding area for whatever supplies we can find among the corpses and in the fields. It is open country, but we return with a bread ball big enough for four people to share, a bolt of linen that might make three blankets, and a bottle of wine for the Commander. It is not much but it is the first food that we have touched for three days."

Arthur's 2nd Division had moved quickly from the front lines on the Ainse River and canal in the Marne department back to Verdun, where they hastily settled into less-than-ideal conditions. Cover was important: recognition by the enemy's aircraft equaled an imminent barrage of artillery shells.

In a new century of new technology, the ways in which that technology was used evolved during the war. In the case of the airplane, tactics changed on the fly, from recon to tactical bombing and air superiority. Skip to Chapter 11 to read more about that. How commanders used tanks evolved, for example, as did how hospitals and recovery units were deployed. Thoughts about the importance of forts and defense in general would change after Verdun and commanders would revisit the concept of offense-at-any-cost after the Battle of the Somme. But battlefield logistics, transportation, and supply tactics evolved as well.

Obviously, a logistics chain to supply the underground forts that protected the city of Verdun must have existed before the German offensive, but once new troops were thrown into the battle, the French Army had to retool its supply lines and schedules for the rotation of reserve and line troops. If a unit was without food and water until then, they had to go without or improvise until the adjustments were in place.

As Arthur wrote his diary, more than 250,000 Frenchmen had amassed in and around Verdun, [70] either in the battle or in reserve ready for it. Every shell, bullet, nail, bandage, mule, lump of coal, or cord of firewood came from and was transported to them from someplace else.

Before the war, everything heavy moved by rail and both France and Germany had among the world's best systems. While applications of the new small internal combustion engine like the car and lorry were becoming more popular and trustworthy, the horse cart was still the mode of choice for local transportation. So, when war broke out, it is not surprising that both the Central and Allied military supply strategies emphasized staging from key depots, with arteries of horse-drawn wagons delivering the necessary equipment, food, and

---

70   *"Siege of Verdun: Supplying the Defenders, 1916, Scientific American, Dan Schlenoff, July 8, 2016, https://blogs.scientificamerican.com/anecdotes-from-the-archive/siege-of-verdun-supplying-the-defenders-1916/*

supplies to the field. [71] While the advantage of a surprise offensive such as the one the German Army organized through Belgium and Northern France in 1914 was, frankly, surprise, the disadvantage of such an effort was the risk of outrunning their own supply lines once they extended beyond practical reach of their key depots. Neither horse nor wagon could keep up. By the end of 1914, essentially a near static trench line had been drawn from the French-Swiss border to the English Channel. The advantage of established battle lines was that predictable supply channels could be created; the disadvantage, of course, being, frankly, stagnation.

Both sides soon developed work arounds and new strategies. Troops knew to dig up, blow up, or disable bridges when the battle required retreat. A month after Germany occupied Belgium, for example, Belgian resistance had so thoroughly sabotaged their own rail infrastructure that reportedly only about 15 percent of the network was operational. [72] Artillery began to saturate and concentrate on supply centers, forcing staging depots to set up seven or eight miles behind the front – the range of the long gun – challenging logisticians to develop ways to close that gap to supply the men in battle. Horses and mules could not make such long trips, so to shorten the distance both French and German supply chains began to rely on 60cm gauge light railway systems. With pre-fabricated tracks similar to today's toy railroads, sections could be brought in, quickly laid down, and then pulled up and relocated as needed. Such tracks were uniform and could be mass-produced, and temporary French and German narrow-gauge networks soon sprang up feeding artillery shells and equipment to smaller supply dumps and refilling points closer

---

71   *"Transport and Supply During the First World War," Mark Whitmore, July 9, 2018. https://www.iwm.org.uk/history/transport-and-supply-during-the-first-world-war*

72   *"Transport and Supply During the First World War," Mark Whitmore, July 9, 2018. https://www.iwm.org.uk/history/transport-and-supply-during-the-first-world-war*

to the front. [73]

As for Verdun, its railway link to Paris had been severed in July 1915, and although a light rail system, or "voie ferree de 60cm" [74] had been constructed, the military and civilian need for supplies and equipment was so great that a new, more robust highway had to be built over the main road leading into the city from the south. [75]

In Verdun today, a bas relief sculpture stands along the Voie Sacree (Sacred Way), a 72km road connecting Verdun to the southerly city of Bar-le-Duc. The highway played a key role in 1916 to supply Verdun and its soldiers during the ten months of the German siege. It is estimated that several thousands of men and 20,000 tons of material traveled back and forth on the road daily. [76] The sculpture by French sculpture Francois Barrios depicts a Corpet-Louvet locomotive engine, various types of military transport trucks, and some of the men who worked tirelessly to keep the system open. The monument marks the point of transfer of supplies from train to muleteers, trucks, and the narrow-gauge rail line that paralleled the road.

An American ambulance driver, Kent Dunlap Hagler, [77] a year later described the Voie Sacree as a road where "half the men of the world were on their way to battle." Of the experience, he wrote:

"This traffic in itself deserves a word in passing. Just north of Erize the great highway begins to branch out

73   "Transport and Supply During the First World War," Mark Whitmore, July 9, 2018. https://www.iwm.org.uk/history/transport-and-supply-during-the-first-world-war

74   Literally "rail line with the width of .6 meters"

75   "Siege of Verdun: Supplying the Defenders, 1916, Scientific American, Dan Schlenoff

76   "List of World War I memorials and cemeteries in Verdun," https://ipfs.io/ipfs

77   Springfield, Illinois, Section Thirty-one, U.S.A. Ambulance Service with the French Army

into the various roads leading to the Verdun front.
Through the town runs the main road from Bar over
which the greater part of the troops and supplies going
to Verdun passed. It was the privilege of my [ambulance]
section to observe this road for many days before the fall
attack of 1917, when cannon of every caliber, from the
tiny trench '37's' to the huge eight-wheeled '220' mortars,
cavalry, engineers, pontoons, artillery, ambulances,
supplies, machine guns, passed by, singly or in convoy a
steady stream of every conceivable means of conveyance
from Rolls-Royces to donkeys. But these were only
incidental to the real traffic of the road --- the endless
lines of troop-laden trucks pressing forward or coming
back. And 'endless' is no idle figure, for during days after
days they passed in double line, a truck every fifteen
yards, twenty-five men to the machine, hour in, hour out,
soldiers all gray with mud or dust, sometimes singing and
sometimes grave, but with an ever-ready greeting for 'les
Américains,' if any of our fellows were in sight." [78]

In a small ironic literary twist to the Battle of Verdun,
to keep the path clear, foot soldiers like Arthur coming to or
leaving the hell on the front lines were not allowed to walk on
the Sacred Road, obliged instead to walk in the fields on either
side.

---

78   *"History of the American Field Service in France," Brigham Young University, http://net.lib.*
byu.edu/estu/wwi/memoir/AFShist/AFS2i.htm

Chapter Eight: "No ambulances"

"We spend the rest of the day digging our trenches, making hardened shelters for the officers, and collecting up the trail of brass cartridges in the ravine. While we are engaged in this work, a caravan of wounded pass by, coming from very close heading to the rescue stations that my regiment is installing in a shelter adjacent to the Colonel's planning room. While we are building the medical station, all that the stretcher-bearers can do is bring casualties in and lay them on the grass. The medical officers bandage the severely wounded, who must then wait for another stretcher-bearer or ambulance to transport them back to the field hospital. The lesser wounded, those who can move out on their own, do not wait. No ambulances come from or go towards Verdun: we can see in the failing light that the Boch have lit up all four corners of the city with their shells. In the evening, the Boch ease up on their shelling of the Thiaumont Farm's orchards so a detail sets out again to replenish our drinking water. By the time we return, it is midnight. We take a little rest to regain our strength, but by then the night has become eerily quiet and it passes into day without too many German annoyances."

At the beginning of the battle for Verdun, the orchards at Thiaumont Farm were a mile or so south of the front and about five miles north of the city. Situated in a small valley west of Fort Douaumont, it must have seemed picturesque that February, snow on leave-less trees waiting for spring. By April, as the Germans fought to occupy Fort Douaumont and the French bravely defended it, the farm was the battlefield front and although the line was to change by several miles as the French lost ground just to the east, the French held their ground at Thiaumont Farm, with maps of the Western Front still crossing through its orchards as late as August 8.

Throughout much of the Battle of Verdun, the Thiaumont Farm was contested ground. In a report by Vixefeldwebel Ludwig Huber of the 1st Bavarian Infantry

Regiment about a patrol he volunteered to make on June 10, 1916, to determine who indeed controlled the Farm, Huber wrote:

> "We marched from the Fosses-Wald to the slope at Douaumont where Lieutenant Hausle called for volunteers to carry out the patrol. The company had already suffered heavy losses in the days before, the men realized that if they were wounded on patrol there would be no coming back. They would have to wait for the Scythe Man to release them from their suffering. In the hell of Verdun, it was up to each man to see that he made it through alive while the roar of enemy guns day in, day out turned forest into field and made our communications trenches almost impassable." [79]

Records show that the French experienced 377,231 casualties at Verdun in 1916, including 162,308 deaths, an appalling ratio of three wounded for every two soldiers killed. [80] In the Battle of the Somme, Germany would see a 6.5:3.5 ratio of casualty vs. killed in action or missing compared to France's 7.8:2.2 ratio. As horrendous as the number appears on paper, the killed vs. casualty ratio could have been worse if not for France's widespread implementation of the battlefield triage process, which they created a century earlier during the Napoleonic Wars to quickly sort, classify, and distribute the sick and wounded. [81] By 1918, after observing France's successes, battlefield triage had become standard in the British

79   "A Soldiers Burden: Thiaumont Farm, June 1916," http://www.kaiserscross. com/40047/132001.html

80   "The Battle of Verdun and number of casualties," http://www.wereldoorlog1418.nl/ battleverdun/slachtoffers.htm

81   "Battlefield Medicine: Triage-Field Hospital Section, George Thompson, University of Kansas Medical Center, http://www.kumc.edu/wwi/index-of-essays/triage-field-hospital-section.html

and American medical corps and today triage is practiced in emergency rooms around the world.

Generally, soldiers along the Western Front needed immediate treatment for one of four injuries: gas, shell shock, diseases, and wounds. For medical staff, time was the enemy. To determine an order for whom to treat first, a medic imbedded in each company would separate his wounded into three categories: the slightly injured, those who needed specialized hospital care, and those beyond help with little chance of survival regardless of available treatment.

In 1916, four identical field hospitals able to accommodate 216 patients each would have been set up six to eight miles behind the front lines, out of the range of enemy artillery. Designed to be mobile, the four units were stationed along major roads leading away from the battlefield.

Later in mid-1918, as a consequence of near-static battle lines, the French grouped all four hospitals and began to assign specialties to each of the four hospitals. One hospital might concentrate on wounded and gassed victims, for example, while another would take the ambulatory sick or those with skin or venereal diseases. One of the hospitals was set up as a convalescent camp, usually run by medical reserve staff. [82]

An early innovation employed by the French medical corps was the methodical approach to the treatment of shock, which affected every wounded soldier to one degree or another coming off of the line. Standard in triage procedures, patients would have been screened and sorted into one of three lines of immediate care: wound dressing, shock, or operation. Treating shock was a top priority, addressed first in the trench or en route, if possible, but certainly immediately upon arrival at the hospital. Treatment for shock ranged from removing wet clothing, providing hot drinks and food, and adjusting

82   *"Battlefield Medicine: Triage-Field Hospital Section, George Thompson, University of Kansas Medical Center, http://www.kumc.edu/wwi/index-of-essays/triage-field-hospital-section.html*

splints and bandages to lessen pain, to administering morphine, intravenous saline solution, or blood transfusions. [83]

Once safely removed by medics and soldiers from the battlefront by stretcher, wounded soldiers were carried to hospitals by ambulance drivers, at first in covered horse-drawn carts like the Mark 1, outfitted to carry two stretchers and eight walking wounded, and later by motorcars capable of carrying four men in stacked stretchers. [84] Medical commanders eventually standardized ambulance designs to include side tent curtains that could be unrolled and staked to the ground as tents, a water tank, medical chest and cupboard for additional stretchers. [85]

Until 1917, before the United States entered the war, American volunteer ambulance drivers in the American Field Service (AFS) were placed under French military control. Under the same military rules and discipline as French soldier, with the same pay and rations, they were among the first Americans to see action in the war. Nearly 2,500 AFS volunteers evacuated more than 400,000 French soldiers during the war and 127 died as a result of their heroism, some from gas, accidents, and influenza, but also from enemy fire. [86]

The AFS was by no means the only ambulance corps carrying Allied wounded from the Western Front. Both the Red Cross and the Salvation Army contributed vehicles and crews.

---

83   ibid

84   *"Air ambulances" were used before WWI in the form of horse-drawn giant stretchers suspended under hot air balloons. The French Air Service, however, is credited with the first use of aircraft after evacuating a Serbian officer from the field to a hospital. (Evolution of the Ambulance, http://firehistory. weebly.com/evolution-of-the-ambulance.html)*

85   *"Provision of Ambulances in the First World War," http://www.salvationarmy.org.nz/our-community/bcm/archives-heritage/articles-collection-provision-of-ambulances-in-the-first-world-war*

86   *"WWI: Remembering the US volunteers who saved French lives at Verdun," Stempanie Trouillad, http://www.france24.com/en/20160218-france-world-war-i-battle-verdun-american-ambulance-drivers-usa*

One notable group was the British-based First Aid Nursing Yeomanry (FANY), an all-female corps of nurses on horseback. Founded in 1907 to reach wounded where ambulance wagons could not go, FANY quickly adapted to WWI conditions, replacing horses and horse-drawn ambulances with motor coaches. It is worth noting, however, that due to British military prejudices against women in battlefield conditions, FANY mostly served French and Belgian divisions until 1916, when they became officially attached to British units. Other British ambulance services that distinguished themselves during the war were the Voluntary Aid Detachment and the Women's Auxiliary Army Corps. [87]

In his memoir "At the Front in a Flivver," ambulance driver and American volunteer William Yorke Stevenson described his 1916 Verdun service:

> "Some twenty huge – at least, they seemed huge to us
> – shells fell around us. This was the heaviest shellfire I
> have yet been under, and I was glad to have something to
> do to keep my mind off of it. Two men about one
> hundred yards away were decapitated and there were a
> number of dead horses about." [88]

87 *"The Women Who Drove Ambulances on the Western Front," Evangeline Holland, The Edwardian Promenade, October 2, 2013, http://www.edwardianpromenade.com/war/wwi-wednesday-women-ambulance-drivers/*

88 *At the Front in a Flivver, William Yorke Stevenson, Houghton Mifflin Company, Riverside Press, Boston, 1917*

Chapter Nine:
"Twenty-two shells a minute"

"After standing in reserve ready for battle in our shelters for a few hours, at midnight we eat a little supper. We are half dead from the cold, our feet numb because for the past five days we have not been able to change our shoes or clean or dry out our equipment. We just wait for the attack. On our side, our artillery is blowing the Boch to rags, but at about 8 a.m. some German planes fly over us again, making us fire our 77mm artillery shells at them. The Boch use the artillery smoke as reference markers, but a stray 105 not intended for us lands in our trees, bursts, kills one of our men and seriously wounds another, who dies soon afterwards. Despite the relatively low number of shells, we lose one sergeant, a corporal, and three men. We start to dig graves and give them a suitable burial but time does not allow us to finish our sad work.

"At 9:30 a.m., the bombardment begins. The shells arrive first two, then four, then six at a time. An officer counts 22 large gauge shells per minute. All we can do is lie down in our holes; we cannot even raise our heads. We remain in this hell waiting for orders. Shells of all sizes are bursting around us and all around us, too, are cries from wounded men calling for medics and stretcher-bearers. Through their pitiful calls we can make out the whirr of the engines from Boch planes overhead coordinating the artillery. On top of all this is the noise of our glorious little 75 guns, which unfortunately by themselves cannot silence the far more powerful German cannons. By tomorrow, they may be demolished but for three days our 75s have blasted the Boch's rear lines and airfields. Without our own planes, however, our heavy artillery is completely ineffective at silencing the enemy's missile batteries, whereas the Boch can continue to draw on us from above.

"From midday until 2 a.m. the Boch have sent shells of all gauges to us, including their 105s, 150s, 210s, 280s, and 320s, which cut indiscriminately through the trunks of large trees and the human bodies that lay below them. We already have about ten soldiers wounded when a

mortar kills three men among us and wounds two others. As each shell arrives, we feel its violent shock and our nerves and muscles tense. Several times between such moments, I say my Act of Contrition and spiritually prepare myself for death because I do not believe that any human being will come out of this inferno alive.

"After about a three-hour lull, the bombardment resumes, this time more violently. A shell falls in the middle of my section, wounds three of my comrades, knocks me to the ground, and throws my rifle in the air. Pieces of my flannel uniform are blown off and what remains of a large tree is on the top of me. I am almost completely buried in the dirt. My first thought is to find better cover so I jump in a shell hole close to me where one of my comrades has just been wounded. Soon after I get him to the rescue station, my Captain is wounded and almost at once so, too, is my Lieutenant.

"The shelling continues to focus on our corner of the battlefield, separating our equipment into their individual parts -- haversacks, snap hooks, pot lids -- so we move further down the ravine and quietly lay low. I find Henri Philippe there, our cycler [messenger] and a good friend of mine. A corporal orders several of the wounded men to carefully make their way as best as they can down the ravine and away from the battlefield. It has been four constant hours of bombardment, and under such violence we are forced to give up our position.

"We crawl down the ravine, then go up to the top of the next one. What we see is astonishing. The Boch's relentless shelling has transformed what had once been the beautiful rolling Haudremont Woods, as lush and bountiful as a set table, into a miserable sight. It is as if a regiment of crazy loggers has just passed through, ravaging the ancient forest into shredded tree trunks. On the ground are blue stains, usually a corpse, and unfortunately, there are a lot of them. By 4:30 in the morning, the attack wains. The Boch must be regrouping because the shells are now falling less on the forces behind the lines and a little more on the front lines. From the top of the ravine we can distinguish those lines by the shell explosions, but our 75s are spitting hard, too, and they make their own devastation on German positions. Through the smoke we can see small groups of Boch tossed about. The few pieces of our artillery nevertheless are expertly aimed and from time to time we can see that some of our gifts are delivered to the German batteries but the Germans can drop more shells than we can, and that is the reason we see so many wounded men pass down the line, especially the Zouaves.

"The Zouaves are in bad shape but when we ask, we learn from them that the Boch counter attack has failed. Some of the Blue Horizon from the 8th and the 160th also pass. We rest for a half hour watching this sad spectacle, then around 5:00 a.m. the firing lessons a little so we go down again into the ravine. We assist where we can, but there are cries everywhere, from the moans of soldiers failing from their wounds to calls for something to drink. Even as they lay dying, some just ask for a drink of water. The earth has been turned over everywhere. Some remains stick out of the ground, some are stuck in the trees. Human parts have been scattered in all directions. I see one gravely wounded soldier trying to put the head back on the body of a comrade who had been alive just a few moments before. We finally make it back to the site where our company was, only to find all of our equipment blown up or turned over and several of our shelters demolished. We combine the remains of several hutments to repair two of them. We find 20 cases of cartridges and gather personal items that are scattered everywhere. We dress the wounds of the soldiers who could not be evacuated during the bombardment, but unfortunately several do not make it. As we can, each person withdraws to take a little rest and make some sense of it. We are able to get a little sleep without the Boch annoying us too badly.

"In one end of the trench, close to the rescue station, our company joins with a company of Zouaves. Lieutenant Colonel Panblan calls for a company roll call: we have one lieutenant, a sergeant, one corporal and 24 men left of the 90 that originally went up the line. We share some watered-down coffee and food with the Zouaves and they share some of their supplies with us. The stretcher-bearers are amazing. We help them as best as we can to evacuate the wounded, because the latter are numerous and some of the stretcher-bearers are in as bad a shape. A good number of them have already received graves for their devotion."

95.

Arthur's combat-hardened regiment had never experienced fighting like this. If it hadn't been for the acceptance that death was imminent anyway, surprise at where the last explosion fell, the instant and irreversible grief at the loss of a friend, the horror of the mangled body in the next hole, or an anticipation of where the next shell would fall – any one of these – the fear would have paralyzed lesser men. Yet, all they could do was try to stay inconspicuous in what might become the grave they dug for themselves. The forest offered no cover – except for some individual trees, there wasn't much of a forest left -- and being in reserve meant that there was no enemy soldier at whom they could fire. Just shells, coming in at the rate of 22 every minute. Only after the shelling had stopped would the company have been able to crawl out and do something, even if it was just to help the wounded.

"Zouaves during a Long Halt," French propaganda post card, Series B, Number 5. Postmarked 1915.

When Lieutenant Colonel Panblan took a roll call to find out how many men he had left, the number wouldn't have included the African Zouaves, who were either fighting as a segregated unit at the end of the trench line or gathered there to regroup as they "passed down the line" towards the hospital station. The Zouave were fierce fighters and either for that reason or because French commanders felt they were expendable as inferior or inexperienced conscripts, they often were the first into battle and took heavy casualties.

Early in the war, the four Zouave regiments of the French Army, known as the Fighting Peacocks, wore their traditional colorful dress into battle but this made them an easy target. The development of the machine gun, rapid-fire artillery and improved small-arms obliged them to adopt a plain khaki uniform in 1915. The Zouaves played a major role in the 1914-18 War with their numbers being expanded to nine regiments de marche. These units retained much of their traditional panache, especially in attack. The first Zouave regiments called up from Africa to France in 1914 for the war were the 8th and 9th, with four additional mixed Zouave and Tirailleur regiments (Régiments Mixtes de Zouaves et Tirailleurs) raised later.

Today, military historians often undervalue the contributions of the Zouave and Senegalese Tirailleurs, colonialists fighting for an imperial ruler, France. Undeniably these soldiers played as critical a role in the ultimate outcome of the war as any of the Allies' lesser-known partners such as Portugal, Romania, and Greece. Today, some Algerians may wonder why their country, a colony that alone gave the conflict 23,000 of its best men, would care to be included in centennial memorial services. [89] In the historic context of the past,

---

89   *"Bastille Day is a reminder of what France owes its colonial soldiers," Ishaan Tharoor, Washington Post, July 14, 2014 (https://www.washingtonpost.com/news/worldviews/wp/2014/07/14/bastille-day-is-a-reminder-of-what-france-owes-its-colonial-soldiers/?noredirect=on&utm_term=.244d534cf151)*

however, it is important to realize that colonists from Algeria, Somalia, Tunisia, Madagascar, Morocco, and Indochina were considered French citizens, and as such given the same rights and privileges under French law as any Parisian. Or Roubaisien, for that matter. To many, such new liberties, responsibilities, and opportunities were well worth the price of colonial subservience.

At first, the ranks of colonial units were filled by volunteers but as the war ran on, authorities imposed forced recruitment and quotas. It is true that most soldiers from the colonies had little desire to fight for France, much less die for her, and the forced conscription in both France and its colonies caused some men who would otherwise be eligible for service to flee to nearby neutral countries. West African chiefs were required to provide a quota to France and most often they turned to their lower social strata for conscripts. [90] To many of these men, it was a chance to jump the boundaries of that strata; to others it was a way out of poverty. For most, serving was an obligation to their family, their chief and to their tribe. [91]

The French poilu from nearly opposite sides of the world had more in common than not. To the conscripted North African Zouave, as well as conscripted Arthur from North France, fighting in the French Army was a duty, and whether they called Tunis or Tourcoign home, soldiers bled the same color in the trenches around Verdun.

---

90   "A Day for the African Army and the Colonial Troops," Library of Congress, https://www.wdl.org/en/item/4593/

91   "The Fighting Peacocks," Military History Now, June 3, 2018, https://militaryhistorynow.com/2018/06/03/fighting-peacocks-the-colourful-history-of-zouaves/

Chapter Ten:
Mules and muleteers

"We learn in the course of the day that we will be raised this evening. I am assigned to take the Grande Rue through Fleury and meet the muleteers bringing us fresh mules, food, and equipment. In exchange, we will hand over our mules, their nets of bundled supply crates completely empty. I leave at nightfall in the fog with the Corporal to get to the appointed site near the Giamont Farm. Our route takes us across that devastated field, with its torn trees and cadavers. Suddenly, we realize that only one of our mules still follows us, the others have strayed in the fog and dark of night. I stay with the mule while the Corporal searches the field but he never finds the animals. Fortunately, our muleteers find us and turn over their mules and much needed cargo. Once we return to the company, we distribute everything and then silently depart this awful place where we have spent so many terrifying hours and lost so many good comrades.

"Our company leaves via the village of Bras, then heads south towards Verdun. By the time we arrive at the barracks in Marceau around 10:00 in the evening, I can barely walk. We get the first restful sleep we have had in two weeks. The next day, the Lieutenant gathers us and from what remains of the Company we form a section. They will head for the front, but I am not going with them. My ankle, wrapped in bandages, is too swollen. Those of us left behind spend the day quietly in relative safety, despite not having any food, but in the evening, some of the muleteers on a supply run (and a little drinking) in Verdun drop by to bring us some potatoes and grains."

Imagine misplacing your rental car just as you are about to turn it back in. Perhaps you're that best man who misplaced the bride and groom's wedding rings. Or imagine that you had a truckload of recycled bottles you'd carried back to the store for a deposit only to suddenly realize that they'd disappeared. That's how Arthur and his corporal might have felt when they realized that the mules they were supposed to return empty and exchange for ones packed with supplies had vanished like lifting fog!

Granted, mules are living, thinking beasts, not machines or mindless glass vessels, and Arthur's mules (he never says how many) found themselves in a dark and quiet field, no explosions, and except for some empty crates, free of their heavy cargo. What's more, they weren't tied together. Even though the mules were trained to stay in line, keep their heads low and follow the ass in front of them, if you were one of these mules, what would you do? Except for the mule in front, which Arthur was probably leading, the others likely took the opportunity to desert.

Along the Front, shelling by long cannon was nearly a daily occurrence. Scheduled bombardments were timed to coincided with infantry charges over the top and intended to push the enemy to the bottom of their own trenches while your side advanced. Often just yards from six-inch howitzers or large cannon throwing foot locker-sized shells across a mile or more of tree-shredded wastelands, the lightning-like flashes and the percussion of air waves slapped man and beast like the flat side of a paddle. [92] The concussion would be accompanied by the general uproar of other guns of various sizes, creating a cacophony of barks, spits, and woofs at a level that made it impossible for men to speak to each other. Depending on the prevailing winds, the smoke would bath the battlefield in purple light, creating weird shadows. Men carrying wounded back from the front lines described later how the hellish sounds and sights would lessen noticeably in intensity step-by-step as the soldiers retreated through the winding valleys towards the field hospitals. [93]

Such conditions were intolerable for humans and lethal to their animals.

---

92   *At a time when hearing protection devices didn't exist, either men improvised with wet cloth or candle wax, or eventually ignored the noise. Perhaps, what later passed as a quiet, sullen, shell-shocked demeanor in Western Front veterans was simple deafness.*

93   *As described by Bert Mackenzie, Canadian foot soldier, in a letter home.*

At the beginning of the war, military policies and doctrine concerning the use of pack animals had yet to adapt to the trench, artillery, and gas challenges unique to WWI. Most horses and mules didn't last long enough to adapt. One British signaler in the 110th Brigade of the Royal Field Artillery was to write later: "We knew what we were there for; them poor devils didn't, did they?" [94]

Often referred to as the Forgotten Army, both the Allies and the Central Powers relied on more than one million – yes, million – mules and horses, [95] to haul trench timber and

94   *"The Forgotten Army," firstworldwar.com, http://www.firstworldwar.com/features/forgottenarmy. htm*

95   *The British Army alone, whose Veterinarian Corps tracked and administered equine inspections, reported the wartime loss of 256,000 mules and horses. In 1917, the worst year of the war to be a British mule, thousands died in the Battle of Arras due to 'the strain of service, the indescribable weather, and the serious curtailment of the oat ration." (Captain Sidney Galtrey, 1919, as quoted in The Forgotten Army, as cited above.)*

"Troops Disembarking," unmailed U.S. post card, H.H. Stratton, publisher

ammunition, food, water, and coal, although to a lesser and lesser degree as the war progressed. Mules and horses served at the Front, in the Rear, and along support and communication lines.

And while we think of the First World War as one that increasingly relied on new war machines, apparently the usefulness of the horse and mule in battle didn't end with that war. In her book The Perfect Horse (Ballantine Books, 2016), Elizabeth Letts mentions that while "most people tend to associate warhorses with World War I, during World War II, the German Army alone used 2,750,000 horses, double the number in World War I." She goes on to write that more than sixty percent of those became casualties of the war, with an average life expectancy of about four years.

In the early years of the first world war, horses and mules were used to bring the heavy shells up to the guns just behind the front lines. Imagine coaxing an animal to follow instructions, much less not bolt, as outgoing shells were fired or incoming shells were bursting around both of you. Behind the trenches, in the supply lines and camps, when the shelling started, horses would back up to their handlers, cringing against the men for reassurance and begging for protection. Unlike the horses, however, mules would often simply stop where they were, regardless of location. This could be quite inconvenient for muleteers who happened to be in muddy ground at the time or who found themselves in the spot being shelled.

Eventually, as larger and larger artillery was brought onto the Western Front battlefield, four-legged transports became obsolete in favor of more powerful and less stubborn tractors, motor vehicles and locomotives but wherever motor trucks and light rail could not go, such as to deliver supplies to Arthur's unit through the shelled and muddy landscape of the Haudremont ravine and the Thiaumont and Giamont farms, the mule and his muleteer were dispatched.

Just as tractors, motor vehicles, and light rail were useless without a steady supply of petrol or coal, horses and mules needed fuel, too: about 25 pounds of grain a day to maintain a healthy weight and physique. With war time food shortages, however, the equine army was typically rationed at 20 pounds of grain a day: 12 pounds of oats, ten pounds of hay and some bran served in a mash once a week. [96]

Finding enough food was just the start of the muleteers' challenges. The animals had to be fed twice a day: early in the morning and then again late at night. They required water in the morning, usually mixed with four pounds of chaff and oats, then they needed more water in the late afternoon. Soldiers assigned the additional duty of muleteer were responsible for knowing what their charges needed and providing it so that the animals were assets, not liabilities, behind and on the battlefield. [97]

In reasonably fair weather, mules and horses could be kept tied to a simple picket line, but in the harsh winters in northern France, slightly warmer paddocks were necessary, although not always available. In the open, wet weather, blankets became sodden and even with frequent rotation, useless. The muleteer learned to strike a balance between clipping or shaving a mule's coat to manage skin disorders and parasites and letting a horse or mule keep its shaggy winter hair.

With their highly-developed senses, battlefield conditions would have been tortuous for mules and horses, which can feel even small insects on their skin and have evolved to root out poisonous plants, moldy grasses, and dirty water. It is worth noting that the mule's pinnae (ears) can turn independently in different directions to focus on noises. Called a Preyer's reflex, their much larger ear flaps can pinpoint a sound's direction and

---

96   "The Forgotten Army," firstworldwar.com, http://www.firstworldwar.com/features/forgottenarmy.htm

97   "Horses and WWI," Ypres 2016, http://www.yprespeacemonument.com/horses-and-ww1/

origin. And although humans hear better than horses below 8kHz, mules excel at higher frequencies: they can hear a 10 or 20 decibel sound (a whisper or rustling leaves) at 50 feet away. Also, a mule's corpus callosum, which transfers information between the two lobes of the brain, is much smaller than that of a human's (relatively speaking), essentially giving it two brains and allowing it to process two sets of sounds from two different ears.

Simply put, the mule had much more sensitive hearing than the muleteer, especially when it came to the high-pitched whine of incoming artillery. [98] Although it could determine with certainty an incoming direct hit long before its handler, like its handler, there was very little it could do about it.

---

98   *"Hearing," David Stang(http://horsesciencehorsesense.com/index.php/hearing/)*

Chapter Eleven: Aerial combat

"*From the potatoes the muleteers brought us, we make French fries. I detach the nets from several horses that the shells recently killed and use my butcher's skills to make steak. Some of our more enterprising scroungers have found some bottles of wine, so we throw it all together and have a leisurely, hot meal. It seems especially good after six days of only monkey meat [99] and stale bread. The Boch continue to send a few shells to us so we avoid occupying any rooms above ground, preferring instead to stay in the basement which we have arranged with bunks, storage, and meeting areas. In the evening, everyone gathers in the Commander's planning room and the CO reads us a note from the General-in-Chief: 'We congratulate the 20th Section and the 1st Section of the 2nd Division temporarily assigned to you.'*

"*We spend a good night in our basement barracks, but the next day, one of our soldiers is killed and another one wounded. The following day at 5:00 in the morning, we leave to wait in reserve in the Souville ravine but it does not take long for the planes to find us again and make our location. We quickly camouflage everything under black tarps and hollow out new holes but twice the Boch's violent shelling forces us to move. We stump the artillerists with our continual movements, but the General does not believe it does any good to keep it up. The planes always seem to locate us eventually anyway. We remain in the ravine two days and two nights without incident but on the third day three more men are seriously wounded and two mules killed so we are forced to move again. We dig deep into the shadows of the right slope of the gully and that appears to quiet things down a little. Then exactly at 3:00 in the afternoon, we see to our great surprise two French planes. French planes! Two new biplanes, each with two engines, and they fly over our new lair and protect us from any surprise appearances from the Clinks [sic]. This boosts our confidence a little but then we spot a black dot drifting in from a distance. We think it is another fighter plane approaching and to our great amazement we*

---

99   *mysterious canned meat, generally unidentifiable, but actually corned beef.*

105.

recognize it as a German Fokker. We can hear it prick and spit as it opens fire. Coming in at the same height of our two heavier machines, one of our planes starts to spiral down. We believe it is hit but it does not crash. It is clear by his skills that the Boch is the better aviator, and with a quick hook he reengages and fires. Our biplane, being heavier and slower than the smaller Fokker, does not return fire. The Boch pilot snipes at it a second time but not wanting to risk crossing our machine guns, he reduces speed, allowing our plane to make a low-level half turn over our lines. Our aviator continues to fly low over our position for a while, but we never see the second biplane again.

"The rest of the day remains curiously calm, and around 10 a.m. on the third day our section, what remains of my company, receives orders to step off the line in reserve. While our men walk back to the ravine in Fleury, I remain with the mules and equipment in the Souville ravine until 4:00 the next morning, then take them to the Marceau barracks where I stay the night."

The trenches in the valley around Fort Souville were particularly contested. In early February, at the outset of the battle, the front lines were miles to the north, providing a buffer from German long guns and preventing a direct bombardment of Fort Souville, Fort Tavennes and the Tavannes Tunnel. But by April with the capture of Fort Douaumont, the Germans had advanced the front lines just a few miles from Fleury, and by August had captured Fleury, establishing the Souville trenches as Verdun's northern line of defense. [100]

Even by April, however, in the Souville Ravine most of the trees and cover were already gone, making it easy for enemy reconnaissance planes to spot and report back to their artillery the precise locations of troops hunkered down in the trenches and ravines. The problem for the French poilu was

---

100   *Map of The Battle of Verdun, http://www.firstworldwar.com/maps/graphics/maps_33_ wfront_verdun_(1600).jpg*

that their side apparently didn't have any aircraft, at least from what Arthur could see. So, when a new kind of French plane appeared in the sky, much less two planes, to fly top cover over the trenches, it had to have been a big morale boost.

In 1916 only two bi-winged, dual engine French aircraft were deployed by the French in the battlefield – the Letord LET and the Caudron G.4-- but the two airplanes that Arthur reported seeing were likely the latter, not the former. The Letord LET reconnaissance bomber was certainly large and unwieldy in a dogfight, but the French only fielded 300 of them so the chances of Arthur seeing one over his ravine might have been slim. Cumbersome in turns, it is unlikely the French would use one to control the skies over Verdun. Besides, the Letord carried three crewmen and Arthur probably would have mentioned a crowd of men in the machine. [101]

More likely, that day Arthur's regiment saw one of the first field flights of the Caudron G.4. By 1916, it was replacing France's G.3, and would have been a distinctive new look, with its four vertical tail surfaces instead of the G.3's two. The new G.4 had two 80-horsepower Le Rhone engines. The two engines gave the aircraft more range and allowed a forward-firing machine gun to be placed center-front. [102] While conventional wisdom might argue that two engines were better than one, something especially true for an aircraft designed primarily as a bomber, in fact, the heavier airframe didn't work so well in a dogfight. Its slow speed and inability to fire to the rear made it more and more vulnerable to German fighters, which were getting lighter and faster. [103]

---

101   *"Letord LET," Military Factory, https://www.militaryfactory.com/aircraft/detail.asp?aircraft_id=1776*

102   *Early on, a tripod-mounted machine gun was placed above the top wing to allow a crewman to shoot to the rear but this proved to be so ineffective that it was often simply removed in operational aircraft.*

103   *"Caudron G.4," Smithsonian Air & Space Museum, https://airandspace.si.edu/collection-objects/caudron-g-4*

German propaganda postcard, "Firing on a German Taube," by T.V. Eckenbrechen, 1914.
Postmarked from Altona, June 5, 1915

Arthur confidently wrote that the German aircraft in this encounter was a Fokker, as if seeing it was not only a familiar sight, but so familiar — perhaps so infamous — that he described it as a distinct aircraft type. It was likely the Fokker E, or Eindecker, single wing, single engine fighter. The Fokker's 100-horsepower engine gave it both power and speed. [104] Introduced in the Fall of 1915 as a scout ship, the Fokker monoplane came equipped with an innovative synchronized machine gun that could fire through the single engine's propeller blades. It wasn't long before German airmen discovered that they could fly, observe, carry a bomb or two, and shoot all at the same time. In this aircraft, German airmen wrote the first book on aerial and air-to-ground combat tactics.

---

104   *"Fokker E," Military Factory, ttps://www.militaryfactory.com/aircraft/detail.asp?aircraft_ id=393*

Chapter Twelve:
Deliverance

"With the afternoon comes new orders, and with a deep sigh of relief we begin to pack up supplies and gather our personal gear. By evening, the rest of the company joins us in Marceau. We leave Marceau immediately to spend the night in the Beveau barracks, and here we are told that our regiment is to stand down. Two days later we leave by car from Glorious to Fery, about 60k from Verdun. My swollen ankle has healed.

"When we unload the cars in Fery, it seems that we have left behind more than just the city of Verdun and its woods and ravines of death. In our dreams, we still hear the shells exploding, but not so violently, and the concussions from our artillery do not sound so extreme in our heads. Slowly, our nightmare in Fleury is passing, and those of us who remain are grateful to have escaped a terrible death. We stay in Fery (which boasts 115 inhabitants!) for four days recovering, then leave for Armice. Three in our group continue to suffer from nerves, two jump at every noise, and all of us worry that the next convoy of trucks we see on the road is coming to find us to bring back to that Haudremont ravine. At the end of fifteen or so days, we leave for Ligny-in-Barrois, where the inhabitants try to make us feel normal and whole again."

Finally, deliverance from the hard fight. Arthur's regiment was relieved and rotated to the rear to spend a few days in the safe barracks behind the lines at Beveau but it is obvious from Arthur's description that his unit had lost a lot of men and the few that remained had been rattled to their core. Beveau is the farthest his unit had been from action since they first set foot in the trenches in April 1915, nearly ten months earlier. Clearly, French commanders had little alternative but to bench the regiment for a while and let them recover.

This brief respite from battle was a time of healing for Arthur's unit, but not all would recover.

It's not hard to imagine, in a superficial way, what must have gone through the minds of the poilu in the trenches and battlements at Verdun. Similar thoughts most certainly were shared by Russian foot soldiers in their ditches on the Eastern Front, their own backs pinned to the proverbial wall in Vilna and Lake Naroch at the time. [105] Sailors in the ships and U-boats on and under the Atlantic Ocean probably were wondering the same thing as they traded rolls back and forth, from methodically-hunting predator to terrified prey: "Can I go on?" or "Can't I just go home?" or maybe "Will I die today?" In every combatant's mind, the instinct to flee is in conflict with the duty to stay.

To this day, how soldiers respond to the impasse between flight and duty defines them. But that definition is situational and evolutionary. A new recruit facing the fear for the first time will usually harden and numb to the threat. Or they might temporarily or permanently become unhinged. A veteran in the field might park the fear deep inside, determined to deal with it in the quiet of some undefined future date or they might temporarily or permanently become unhinged, too.

During WWI, this fear haunted both officer and soldier every day, but especially in 1916 and 1917, as offensive and defensive combat stagnated into what seemed like endless days of useless, inevitable brutal violence. The mental pressure and physical strain of daily tasks; seeing comrades maimed, eviscerated, or killed; the nauseating smells and sights; the concussive force of the obus; and trying to make sense of it in what was supposed to be an enlightened age at the turn of a new century cracked even veteran soldiers. Soldiers were said to have developed "hysterics." To medical staff, officers, who were presumed to have more control over their situations and therefore assumed to suffer milder causes, were said to have

---

105   *An Allied offensive on the Eastern Front that was swiftly defeated by the Germans at the cost of 70,000 casualties (http://www.historyplace.com/worldhistory/firstworldwar/index-1916.html)*

contracted "neurasthenia." Commanders just called it all "shell shock."

No one could predict either their own or their comrades breaking point but it was terrifyingly clear that every man had one. Evidence of it assaulted the soldier in the trench every day. Perhaps because of the sheer number of cases, however, for the first time, doctors and medics began to seriously examine psychiatric casualties as diagnoseable and treatable cases. As early as 1915, when the term "shell shock" was first coined by British physician C.S. Meyers, [106] six categories of triage and sorting began to be applied to those suffering from "war neurosis" cases: shell fright, gas fright, hysteria, mental or physical fatigue, malingering, and cowardice. [107]

Treatment given to war neurosis ranged from indifference, sympathetic listening, hypnosis, psychotherapy, to electroconvulsive shock therapy. The use of electrodes to stimulate paralyzed limbs became more accepted as the war progressed, although not without controversy. In Germany and France, extending this practice to shell-shocked patients was common place, and according to a number of respected neurophysiologists, it seemed to work quite well. Many who went through such treatment, however, were not so certain. [108]

106   The Great War, Jay Winter and Blaine Baggett, Penguin Books USA NY, NY, 1996, pg. 212

107   "Battlefield Medicine: Triage-Field Hospital Section, George Thompson, University of Kansas Medical Center, http://www.kumc.edu/wwi/index-of-essays/triage-field-hospital-section.html

108   "Battlefield Medicine: Triage-Field Hospital Section, George Thompson, University of Kansas Medical Center, pg. 213 http://www.kumc.edu/wwi/index-of-essays/triage-field-hospital-section.html

Chapter Thirteen:
Redeployment west

"We leave Ligny-en-Barrois and drive through the night towards Groins. When we get to Mezy in the morning (close to Chateau-Thierry), we leave the cars and walk to Rosy where the civilians host us in quiet and clean but small houses. They treat us well. We spend 15 days there, and I am able to take several walks in the beautiful Faulgone Wood. It is a good time. The unit leaves for Fismes, where we bunk down for three nights in an old slaughterhouse, preparing to be called back up for battle. When the regiment finally goes up the line, it is near Paissy. On the front they sleep in caves. Normally, the Boch can spot us from above but in the caves we do not have anything to fear from either their artillery or the bombs they drop from their airplanes. My section remains in reserve in the village for eight days, then take our assigned place in the front-line trenches. Unlike some, we have a good sector: the trenches are well built and the land between us and the Boch is wide and well defended. I am assigned to be the liaison officer on the Lieutenant's staff, which means I sleep and eat regularly, since my bunk is close to the HQ planning rooms in small but fortified shelters. In this roll, I help deliver orders to front line and reserve units. After a while, I am tapped to go to Borough and help train the new troops how to avoid being killed by Boch machine gun fire. Done, I am granted a few days leave and when I return, I report back to my commanding officer at Paissy, who is now in charge of the entire section.

"It is April 23, 1916, Easter Sunday. I assist with mass to both celebrate our commander's promotion and pray for our future. My unit's job is to protect the right flank, but the sector remains quieter than usual because the German lines are at least 800 meters away from us. When we stand down, we spend several days at a farm called Mal-Batu in Vendesse-Beaulne, which still has 1500 or more crates of legumes unharvested in the fields. The heroic civilians are there still working! We leave Vendresse to spend one night in Bauval, before taking off again to camp at a farm in Eguysi, close to the village of Aouny. In their harvested fields during the *day, we practice maneuvers and march a lot but in the evening we serve as voluntary field hands helping bring in crops. For our help, the inhabitants feed us well and I learn about fifteen new recipes.*

"We leave Eguizy for Coulonge and from there we travel through Fere-in-Tardenois to return to the Somme. It takes us a night and the next day on the train to make the trip, getting off around 2:00 in the morning at Saleux, seven kilometers south of Amiens. We help unload artillery shells from the railcars, then leave to join the rest of our division in Revel, a few miles west and a little more south from Amiens than Saleux. For 15 days we remain well-quartered in the homes of the fine people in Revel, and their simple but very French way of living reminds us constantly of what we are fighting for."

The trip from Ligny-in-Barrois to Mezy-Moulins covered about 120 miles, or about the very limit the regiment could have traveled in a day. This took Arthur from the quiet of the countryside south of Verdun where his unit was recovering, north and east to the Marne River, within sight of Reims. In a matter of a few weeks, they had settled into the trenches at Paissy, north of the Marne River and just north of the border between the Marne and Ainse departments. About 40 days passed between the time Arthur's unit left the chaos in the Souville Ravine east of Verdun and when they set up in the relatively orderly trenches north of Reims. If they saw any action, Arthur does not report it, either because it was relatively quiet or because France's commanders were building up troop strengths farther west. When his regiment stood down from the front lines, it was moved to Revelles to join up with the rest of the division.

Arthur reports that his regiment was quartered on a farm struggling to bring in their harvest. In late April, the farmers would be pulling from the ground late winter-tolerant, early spring legumes, such as leafy greens, peas and broad beans, broccoli, cauliflower, shallots and garlic, and root vegetables such as parsnips, beets, and swedes (rutabagas). After a brutal winter, the planting would have been late and the growth modest at best.

Not surprisingly, beginning in 1914 after the general call-up of young men right at harvest time, food shortages and rationing begin to pop up. Then, with the loss of prime farmland in France's north and a growing shortage of fertilizers and machinery, the country's agricultural production plummeted. [109] Harvesting during the war years was a task for old men and their wives and daughters, who presumably worked longer hours across several of their neighbor's fields to do what they could to bring in the wheat and other grains, legumes, sugar beets, and potatoes needed to both serve the war effort and survive the winter.

Arthur's unit helped them bring in that harvest, not just as an entertaining release and because France must eat: his unit needed to practice maneuvers in the farmers' fields in preparation for whatever his commanders were planning next.

---

109   *The First World War 1914-1918, Gerd Hardach, University of California Press, Berleley and Los Angeles, 1977, pg. 131*

Chapter Fourteen: Preparations

"Several times I have walked the 14 miles to Amiens, but this time I leave Revel in a car to help prepare for a new camp along the Somme. Its barracks are poorly built and there are not enough of them. It rains so much, yet we must assemble our fabric tents. We spend eight days there. The guns' firing count now is extreme: the beginning of the offensive should not be far off. We leave for Chipilly, and on the way we meet some cooperative prisoners who tell us that we have to attack."

It was late May or early June 1916. Six months earlier, French Commander in Chief General Joseph Joffe had proposed to British military leaders that the Allies launch a German battle of attrition to draw out German reserve units. British commanders agreed with the strategy in principle and proposed an August attack in or around the open flatlands of Flanders in Belgium. The German attack on Verdun in February, however, forced a change in both location and timing. To compel German commanders to counter with troops from nearby Verdun and provide the beleaguered fort some relief, General Joffe argued for and the Allied army chiefs agreed to an earlier date and to focus the offensive in the Somme, where the British and French lines converged. The offensive was designed to deploy French and British forces equally but with French losses mounting at Verdun, the British agreed to take point. [110]

That's not to say the French were absent at the Battle of the Somme. On the contrary, with his HQ in Dury, French 20th Army Corps commander Ferdinand Foch and his staff had been meeting with British commanders to organize a coordinated battle strategy.

---

110   *"Battle of Somme," William Philpott, Encyclopedia, https://encyclopedia.1914-1918-online. net/article/somme_battles_of*

This dual command, however, complicated the organization and preparations for battle. [111] The Allies needed to establish logistics delivery systems if there was to be any hope of sustaining an offensive. Although the French Army could use their existing infrastructure, the British would need time to build a supply chain to support the nearly 400,000 men and 100,000 horses; gather the necessary equipment, munitions, rations, and supplies they would need, and then move it all into place. [112]

Arthur's unit had been moved into the Somme in early May in anticipation of an offensive, but it is likely that the multilateral military coordination kept it in a state of limbo until a date was announced. For much of the summer, his regiment remained camped and ready in Revelles, southeast of Amiens, and presumably as other regiments arrived the camp got more and more crowded. Despite the heavy rain, many who might normally have been assigned dry beds in barracks found themselves in soggy tents. Perhaps to relieve overcrowding as much as to pre-position units, Arthur's regiment walked or drove to Chipilly, establishing a camp on the north bank of the Somme about 15 miles up-river from Amiens.

In the days leading up to July 1, the British began an intensive artillery barrage hoping to soften German positions. The French divisions supporting the campaign along its southern flank began to fire their artillery a few hours before the appointed push was scheduled. [113] On July 1, 1916, the British attacked with fourteen divisions, the French with five, initiating what would be called the controversial Battle of the

111   *"The French Army in the Battle of the Somme," The Somme Centenary, http://www.somme-battlefields.com/somme-first-world-war/french-army-battle-somme*

112   *"The Long, Long Trail," Battle of the Somme, http://www.longlongtrail.co.uk/battles/battles-of-the-western-front-in-france-and-flanders/the-battles-of-the-somme-1916/logistical-preparations-necessar*

113   ibid*

Somme. Arthur's regiment was presumably still building up its numbers from units that could be spared from the defense of Verdun and in the meantime, it stood in reserve. In early September, the French 10th Army, including Arthur's division, under General Joseph Micheler joined the battle for the Somme with an attack on a 20-kilometer front to the south of the Ainse River in an attempt to extend the offensive to the southern front lines. [114]

---

114   "Battle of Somme," William Philpott, Encyclopedia, https://encyclopedia.1914-1918-online. net/article/somme_battles_of

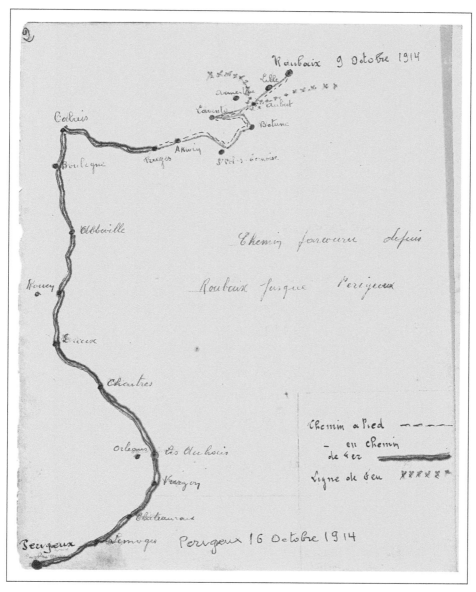

Map 1, hand drawn, "Journal de Route depuis mon depart de Roubaix, 9 Octobre 1914 jusqu'a mon retour 21 Aout 1919," Arthur Dumoulin, page 2.

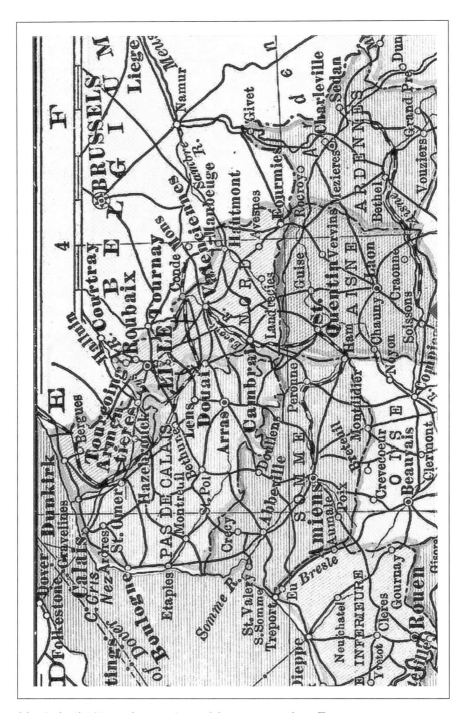

Map 2, detail, 1914 road map, regions and departments, northwest France

120.

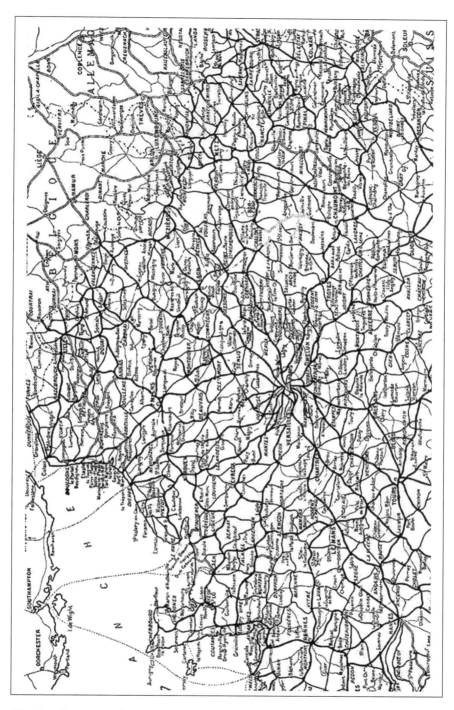

Map 3, rail system, northern France, 1914

121.

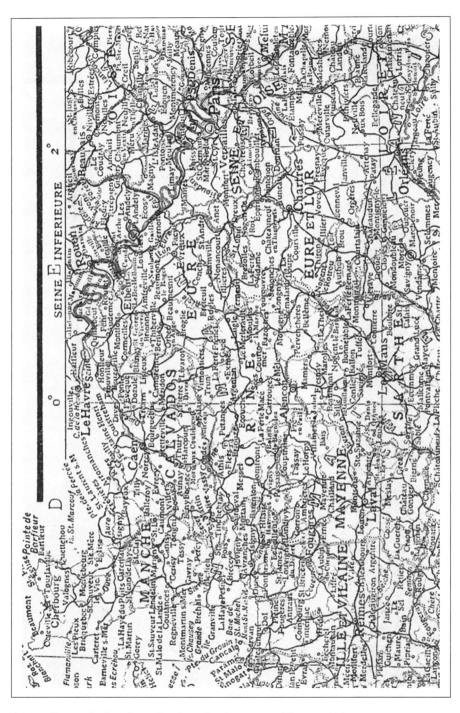

Map 4, Rouen, the Oise, Paris. Roadmap detail, west-central France, 1920

122.

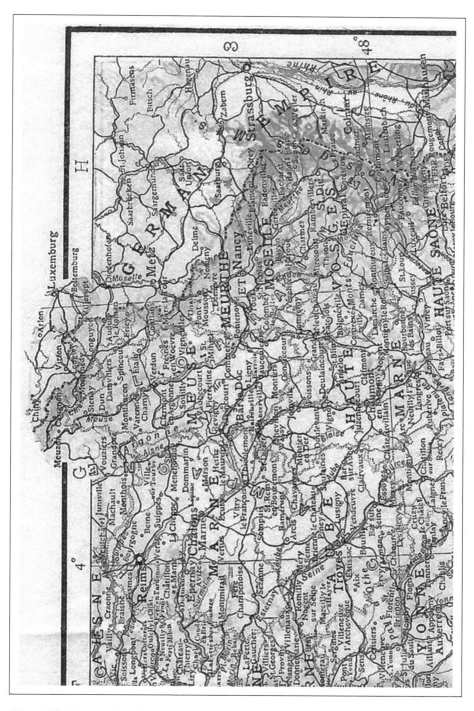

Map 5, The Marne and the Meuse. Roadmap detail, northeast-France, 1920

123.

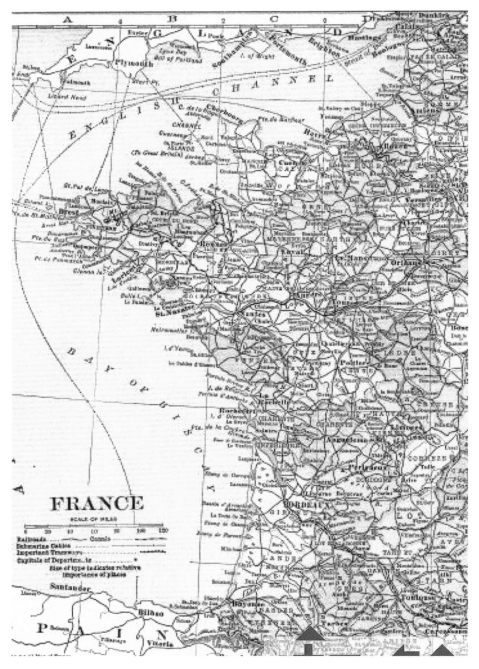

Map 6, England, France, Spain, 1920

124.

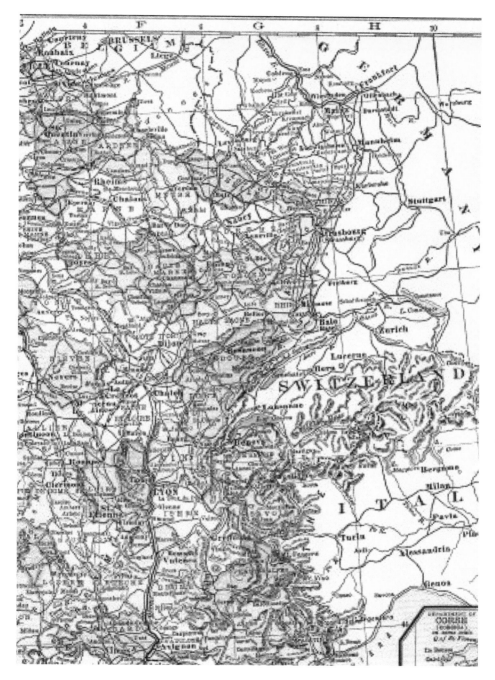

Map 7, Belgium, Germany, Switzerland, Italy, 1920

125.

INFANTERIE
1917

"The Infantryman, 1917," French propaganda postcard, Military Illustration, Series 1, Number 17

PART FOUR:
FIELD OF ASYLUM TO THE SOMME,
SEPTEMBER, 1916 to APRIL, 1917

Fought between July 1 and November 1, 1916, historians still debate the wisdom and effectiveness of the Battle of the Somme. The Allied offensive was timed and designed to relieve pressure on Verdun, so it made sense for the British to take the point but on the first day of battle they suffered more than 57,000 casualties, including 19,240 soldiers killed. [115] On the first day! By the official end of the battle in November, the Allies and Central Alliance together lost more than 1.5 million men. [116]

As Arthur's diary attests, the British and French offensive to recover the farmlands and villages that bordered on or around the valleys and ravines sloping into the Somme River were an ebb and flow of gained and lost ground. The very nature of trench warfare made the role of the infantrymen in the trenches key to advancing and holding ground, or what British Lieutenant General Sir Henry Rawlinson referred to as "bite and hold" tactics. [117] Essentially, at its core, however, the Battle of the Somme was a battle of artillery.

What drove the infantrymen into trenches early in the war was the artillery shell, not the machine gun. "L'obus" shells came in all shapes and sizes, often delivered in barrages that could last for hours. Shells might range in size from the 75mm French "Distribution" or the German 77mm "Meow" and "Zim-Boom" (no translation needed) light shells to the heavies, such as the 150mm Gros Noir, the 280mm "le Charles Humbert," and the

---

115   *The Somme, Peter Hart, Pegasus Books, NY, pg. 528*

116   *Some scholars mark the ending date of the Allied offensive in the Somme well into December so the number of casualties could be higher.*

117   *The Somme, Peter Hart, Pegasus Books, NY, pg. 25*

305mm nicknamed "le train de permissionnaire," or the Furlough Train.

At the start of the war, both sides used shrapnel shells, a devastating weapon when used on advancing troop in open ground. The shrapnel shell was designed like a giant shotgun shell, with disbursing metal or bullets in the front and two fuses in the back, one a time fuse, the other a percussion fuse. Ideally, an experienced artillerist would set the time fuse to explode just before impact, spreading shrapnel from overhead to shred barbed wire, wooden posts, or attacking troops.

If the timing wasn't right, however, the percussion fuse

Empty brass shell casings and crates line the road during the Allied shelling of German positions, Battle of Remy Ridge, France, 1917 (Photo courtesy www.worldwar1archive.com)

would detonate the shell on impact. Unfortunately, or fortunately, depending on what end of the shell's trajectory a soldier was standing, a percussion fuse usually advanced the shrapnel faster in the direction it was already going. In other words, a percussion fuse often simply drove the shrapnel more or less harmlessly into the ground. [118] And so, the idea of trench protection was formed.

In a way, artillery time and percussion fuses set the scene of battle in WWI. Logistics and supply systems had to be created and tracks laid for rail lines to support the heavy shells and their larger and larger guns. Experienced artillerists were required, dictating extensive training to hone timing and rates of fire. Spotters, both on high ground and in the air, were necessary to provide locations and feedback for adjusting a gunner's aim. The critical spotter function drove battlefield decisions and tactics and seeded doctrine for such roles as the forward controller, field communications, and air support. Shelling tactics centered around short-range offensive uses, to cut barbed wire in advance of an infantry charge, for example, or long-range defensive uses, such as to destroy or drive back the opponent's artillery.

Along the Front in the Somme valley, the British brought up 427 heavy artillery pieces, spacing them an average of 30.7 meters apart along their nearly 20-mile span. Surely, nothing could survive such a carpet of shelling that the British laid down on the German side of the front lines in the days before the offensive began.

Right?

Well, unfortunately, the Battle of the Somme revealed some shortcomings of the British Army's "traditional" uses for artillery. Forget that British and French security was lax and the Germans knew precisely when the July 1st attack was to happen. Forget that blanket carpeting of British shelling predictably preceded an infantry attack, all but eliminating the element of

---

118   *The Somme, Peter Hart, Pegasus Books, NY, pg. 49*

surprise. Forget, too, that heavy guns and heavy shells require heavy logistics to bring both weapon and ammunition within range of the enemy. In the Battle of the Somme, deep British shelling of the rear trenches left intact many barbed wire obstructions and German machine gun teams in the first trenches. Without adequate reconnaissance and intelligence about how effective their shelling had been, British soldiers charging out of their trenches were cut to pieces. Following the deadly first day, seasonal rains and regional fog made intelligence gathering via field observations even more difficult. As a result, the British efforts in the Somme from July until September were essentially a hecatomb.

While the British offensive attacked north of the river, the French attacked on the south. The French, with their experience fighting the German Army at Verdun, faired a bit better, advancing a little closer to their objectives than their allies. But like the British, after the first few days the conflict became a battle of attrition.

The British launched their Battle of the Somme offensive on July 1, but Arthur's regiment did not engage in the battle until early September. His division essentially arrived at the Battle of the Somme late but stayed to clean up after the ball, manning the trenches not only into the bitter winter but participating in the Battle of Craonne in April the next year.

Chapter One: Prisoners of war

"We stay close to the airfield and assist as best we can the many flights departing for missions over enemy lines. Even though the prisoners arrive in small groups, by now they number at least 5000, including many officers, even a German colonel. We are ready and in fact are ordered to advance to the front but it is too dangerous so against orders we are forced to wait and only leave the following day."

-- September 3rd, 1916

Prisoners of war have presented logistical, political, and humanitarian challenges to warring armies since the beginning of recorded time. On early Greek and Roman battlefields, to surrender in battle meant certain execution or enslavement. [119] In a modern and more enlightened era, at least in times leading up to the First World War, the closest thing to international rules for the treatment of prisoners of war were dictated by the 1st and 2nd Geneva Conventions of 1864 and 1906 and the Hague Conventions of 1899 and 1907.

In a nutshell, the Geneva and Hague conventions gave the sick and wounded, medical staff, and chaplains neutral status and they recognized safe passage for evacuation convoys and hospital ships. The closest that the language came to addressing non-wounded prisoners of war (POWs), however, was to respect the authority of a prisoner's rank among his peers during interment or capture. In 1916, Germany and Russia agreed to the Stockholm Protocol, which set down a procedure for exchanging prisoners, especially the physically and mentally ill. Later in the war, the Netherlands and Switzerland offered

---

119   *"The Enslavement of War Captives by the Romans to 146 BC," Jason Wickham, May 2014, https://web.archive.org/web/20150524213405/http://repository.liv.ac.uk/17893/1/Wickham]_May2014_17893.pdf*

neutral POW camps to alleviate overcrowding. [120] After examples of inhumane WWI prisoner camp conditions received public attention, however, including a number of atrocities on both sides, general language about POWs was internationally recognized as part of the Third Geneva Convention in 1929.

Today, an army is expected to take reasonable care of those who are forcibly or voluntarily removed from combat but going into WWI both the Allies and Central Powers were held to but a few loose standards.

During the first world war, lasting across five years with blood shed on the soil of three major continents, a reported 10 million people, both servicemen and civilians, were captured and sent to detention camps. [121] Arthur made his diary notation in September, 1916 about the prisoners of war he'd seen in the Somme, but even as early as the winter of 1914-15, just six months into the war, more than one million soldiers had already been taken as prisoners. With no end in sight and the number of prisoners mounting, it was clear on both sides of the Front that the number of POW camps had to be expanded. With the rapid expansion, however, conditions within the camps varied depending on country, staffing and facilities, camp location, and rank. [122]

It is likely that many of the prisoners Arthur saw as his unit waited to be called up north of the Somme River would have been sent to one of 74 different prisoner of war camps in France, although Italy ran 11 and England 13. The Allies also staffed 64 detention camps in French and British colonies in

---

120   *"Prisoners of the First World War, the ICRC archives," ICRC Archives, https://grandeguerre. icrc.org/*

121   *"Prisoners of the First World War, the ICRC archives," ICRC Archives, https://grandeguerre. icrc.org/*

122   *"Find your ancestors," Find My Past, https://www.findmypast.com/articles/world-records/full-list-of-united-kingdom-records/armed-forces-and-conflict/prisoners-of-war-1914-1920*

Africa. [123]   Nearly 7000 Germans and Austrians were even
detained in Australia, most for "crimes of family descent," a
euphemism for being imprisoned for simply having immigrated
to Australia from a historically-Germanic or Prussian country.
[124]

In most camps, civilian detainees and captured
combatants were housed in separate units and generally, camps
also segregated men by their nationality. Daily life for prisoners,
however, was surprisingly similar across most of Western
Europe. Days started with a roll call and sometimes mass
exercises. Mail call and meals were the high points; forced labor
and camp chores, perhaps, the low points. Some larger camps
and camps for officers might include exercise yards for sports,
and even supervised group walks into town. Those who worked
generally had one day off a week for rest.

Trying to tie together a common humanitarian policy
across both sides in the war was the International Committee
of the Red Cross (ICRC), which set up a Prisoner of War
Agency almost at the very beginning of the war. Furthermore,
the International Red Cross was charged with inspections and
documentation of prisoners and prison conditions almost by
default as an outgrowth of its responsibility to monitor the sick
and wounded. [125] This would not have been an unreasonable
default for the Red Cross to assume: more than half of the
Russian casualties on the Eastern Front, for example, came
from among men who were taken prisoner. [126] When a

---

123   *"Prisoners of the First World War, the ICRC archives,"* ICRC *Archives, https://grandeguerre.
icrc.org/*

124   *"Australia's forgotten WWI prisoners," Jessica Campion, July 5, 2011, Australian Geographic,
http://www.australiangeographic.com.au/topics/history-culture/2011/07/australias-forgotten-wwi-
prisoners/*

125   *"Find your ancestors,"* Find My Past, *https://www.findmypast.com/articles/world-records/full-
list-of-united-kingdom-records/armed-forces-and-conflict/prisoners-of-war-1914-1920*

126   *The Pity of War, Ferguson, Niall, London 1998, pg. 368*

soldier was reported missing in action, the Agency attempted to work through official channels to locate him as a prisoner of war. Even in remote locations like Burma and Algeria, it arranged for prisoner of war camp inspectors and forwarded letters to and from POWs to family, including care packages. The Agency lobbied the governments on both sides, advocating for humane treatment and legal rights under international and moral laws. [127]

Detail, French propaganda postcard, "Prisoners of War, 1914. Convoy of German prisoners leaving for Morocco aboard the 'Montreal.'" Postmark: none.

---

127   "Prisoners of War," Heather Jones, International Encyclopedia of WWI, (https:// encyclopedia.1914-1918-online.net/ article/ prisoners_of_war)

Chapter Two: Maurepas by night

"We leave by car from Chipily, arriving at Bronfay Farm between Brays-Nap and Maricourt. We take our equipment to the rear and establish ourselves at the exit of Maricourt. but as we have orders to engage the Boch, we enter the village from the south by the main road between Carnoy and Maricourt and wait through the night for our turn to go up to the front lines. Around 10:30 in the morning, we receive the order to march up to the south side of the village of Maurepas, where we are to stand in reserve, ready. We leave Maricourt, pass through Hardecourt, and arrive in Maurepas at 3:00 in the morning.

"A liaison officer meets up with our unit as we leave Maricourt. He leads and in silence we key on his lantern so that we do not lose our way in the night. We see the lights of Hardecourt and walk just north of the village. It is necessary for us to climb palisades and to jump over trenches in the dark and at one point I miss my dash and I fall into a rather deep hole. Fortunately, I have my helmet on, for without it the cartridge cases I am carrying would have split my head open. We arrive at our appointed spot on the right side of Maurepas, exhausted to the point where we can no longer stand upright any more. In fact, several in our unit cannot keep up, and catch up later. We sleep in the trenches, beating off the flies in some of the trench shelters spared by the Boches' terrible bombardment. We remain on the line in those trenches for three days, after which the other half of our division comes back to relieve us and our regiment rotates back into reserve. We fall back to "Firm Red," where we take shelter in some decrepit cabins in the middle of the English heavy batteries. The British long guns, the Frenchwomen, don't stop firing through the night, rattling our already weak shelters and preventing us from sleeping, but also attracting a continuous barrage of Boch return fire."

It was early September, 1916, and Arthur's unit had been part of a joint British and French push north.

Allied units deployed from Bonfray Farm, an immense

German post card, "In the Trench," Schaar & Dathe, publisher

136.

unified camp with few hard shelters but acres upon acres of cloth tents and temporary structures made of whatever material units could find or bring in with them: planks, boards from crates, tree trunks or branches. It covered several hundred hectares, described by one soldier later as a "human anthill." Day and night, the roads that crisscrossed through Bonfray carried convoys of cars, heavy artillery, columns of marching reserve soldiers and those coming off of the line, as well as ambulances and trucks carrying materiel, munitions, food and supplies from the railhead in the Farm to every direction of the compass. [128]

Maricourt was on the edge of the British front during the Battle of the Somme. As such, the liaison Arthur wrote about might have been a British soldier coordinating with the French army [129] but likely Arthur referred to a French soldier who is assigned duty was to coordinate communiques between units in the field and deliver mail and messages, including new orders, to the various units assigned to recapture or hold the small villages, farms, and hills north of the Somme.

By the time that Arthur's unit marched northward through Maricourt, Hardecourt, and Maurepas, these once quaint, rural, unassuming communities were but reference points on a map, their rubble piled up in the rough approximation of village buildings after battles two years earlier. As such, it is amazing that there were lights on at all in any of the three villages. A Territorial British solder from India described the Maricourt of 1916:

"We came here last night. The town is Maricourt or rather it was, because Maricourt, once a large village of

---

128   *"Poilu, Louis Barthas, translated by Edwrd Strauss, Yale University Press, pg. 256-257*

129   *"The French Army in the Battle of the Somme," The Centenary, http://www.somme-battlefields.com/somme-first-world-war/french-army-battle-somme*

well to do farmers is but a pile of ruins such as I never thought I would see. I didn't see a single house still standing, and apparently there were many hundreds of them at one point. Farms, shops, workshops, the church, the big, square, solid church, have been victims of shells and fire. Nothing living remains here, except a cock, which I was surprised to hear announcing the frigid dawn. In the streets that we passed through, we had to go in single file because of the collapsed walls that blocked them. All the efforts of generations were devastated, roofs torn off, showing their timbers, doors torn off their hinges and blackened by fire, walls that contained nothing any longer. The debris is such that one wonders if the returning inhabitants will find enough energy to undertake the clearing and the rebuilding of this mass of rubble." [130]

After at least three days and nights of hard fighting under punishing concussive artillery, Arthur and his unit were exhausted. The second half of their division rotated into the trench and Arthur and his comrades marched away from the new front, taking some relative rest in British trenches along the "Firm Red" line, the original British trenches and shelters built prior to the July 1 outbreak of the battle. Behind these original lines, established British artillery gun sites continued to launch shells overhead, shells that were traveling miles into German-held territory, possibly as far as the Hauderlu Woods and perhaps Combles.

---

130   *"In the Trenches: A First World War Diary," Pierre Minault, translated by Sylvain Minault, "Not Even Past," notevenpast.org, Department of History, University of Texas - Austin, Nov. 16, 2014*

Chapter Three: Over the top

"We remain in the middle of this din during September 8 and 9. I make coffee for the unit and cook horse bifsteaks for them in an English helmet. On the 10th, we are called back to the French trenches and attack in two waves, charging ahead like crazy men through the front line at Maurepas. We leave many fresh corpses unburied on the ground behind us and we recover a little ground, but it takes us all of September 11th to do it. In the evening, we begin digging a new trench to hold the field, a large plain of dead bodies that in the September heat have begun to decompose.

"At four in the morning, the new trench is ready and we take up our positions in it, only to be told to expect to leave at noon the next day. For two days our artillery has continued to fire on Boch positions directly in front of us. By 11:30 everyone has their orders: we must go over the top of the trench precisely at 12:30. Our objective is the Hauderlu Wood and the hospital and the farm beyond. On schedule, at 12:20 in the afternoon, the spotter airplane flies over us to direct the artillery. Ten minutes later it drops a flare to let the division's troops along the line know when to charge. Eventually, it drops another to let us know when to stop. With the second flare, we take cover in a ravine. During the fighting, we have slowly moved to the left which luckily carries us away from where the Boch think we are. We are able to advance since the artillery has not found us and the machine gun is concentrating on the part of the ravine where we were. The first wave that reaches the top of the woods doubles back and soon stops the Boch resistance in the trench by the hospital. We concentrate on securing the ravine.

"We killed some and some of ours are killed but all in all, we do not take too many casualties.

-- September 12th, 1916

Chapter Four: Hauderlu Woods

"We are well protected by a rocky ridge on our left as we pass through the Hauderlu Wood along the front line. We sneak out of sight of the German 77m artillery batteries, and pass the bunkers where a few Boch gunners are still hiding.

"In the bottom of a shell hole we come across two Boch soldiers, one with his arms around his companion. We find them by their lowing, defeated cries to surrender, their faces the faces of men turned into idiots from the noise of the guns and shells falling around them for two days. We pass them down as prisoners. We arrive at the end of the ridge that protects us, but as we emerge from the overhang a Boch machine gun perched in a crevice starts to open fire on us. Its focus is the 9th Company on our left, but it does some serious damage to some men in my company, too. We receive the order to lay down and crawl to a small embankment 100 meters opposite us and hold our position. We arrive there in stages, some shooting at the machine gun nest while others approach. When we get close enough, we fire on the Boch position and silence it. For the victory, we have to bury a sergeant from the 10th Company that my friend Ausnat knew. We dig holes to spend the night in under the shelter of larger embankments on the left and the right.

"At 3:00 a.m., orders are sent to us from the 1st Battalion to proceed with the plan to take the hospital trench. As we advance, we lay down some counter fire to annoy the Boch line so that they will leave the 1st Battalion alone on the left but after a hundred meters we come to a place at the end of the trench where it meets our ridge. We groan when we see it is topped with barbed wire that our artillerists missed. The Boch who occupy the trench open up heavy fire on us with their rifles and machine-guns which claim some of us. A company of Zouaves slightly ahead of us on a ridge see our difficulty and knowing that we need to advance, attack the Boch from behind with a grenade attack. The German soldiers, realizing that they are pinned on both sides and are about to be taken prisoner, prepare to surrender but the 1st Battalion which they have been slicing up all day

are not in a forgiving mood. The 1st open up a violent volley which reduces to just a score the number of the prisoners that they would have taken. We take the trench but in the middle of the second attack we lose Colonel Brousseau, and Loze and Castel, two nice men from Toulouse in our company.

"By evening, we have secured 800 meters of empty trenches between us and 110th who have been cut off. In three places in the trench we install machine guns to create a crossfire and expect a Battalion from the 33rd to come up shortly to occupy the line. We send some of our company ahead for reconnaissance and they report that all of the Boch have left. The battalion arrives the next morning. We hand over the ravine defenses to them and move on to our next objective.

"A Boch machine-gun that we believe is perched in an electric transformer shack on the main road between Combles and Sailly-Saillisel hinders our approach to the farm. We tell the 27th Artillery about it and by the third 75mm shell, the transformer is gone. Around midday, our troops attack the farm which is heavily defended. After the second try, we can see the men leaving out the back, but soon one of our rockets, then another, hits the farm house and the silence between spits of resistance gunfire lengthens, then stops. The farm is taken.

"It is 1:15 in the afternoon. The road through the of Hauderlu Wood is secure. We have taken the hospital trench and the farm beyond. All our objectives have been reached."

Chapter Five: Sailly-Saillisel

"In the evening we return to the trench to help reconstruct the hospital shelter. Our Company stands ready in reserve but we are not in the action. We do receive a few Boch artillery shells but they do not land close to us. We spend several days in our hole, then we are called back to the front trenches along with the 43ième who, with us, are the last in the fray.

"Our company goes with Lt. Peleton in the direction of Leforest. By following the White Cord, we arrive without too much difficulty on the road that leads to Maurepas. At the agreed gathering point, we stop to eat a little bread, a hard-boiled egg, and some hot coffee. We eagerly consume it: for several days we have had little to eat and what we did eat was always cold.

"We walk through Maurepas and Hardecourt, and at Maricourt we begin to set up a full camp, assembling our tents and anticipating a good night's sleep. We are able to clean up a bit, but we have neither clean clothes nor linen, the bags of those are with the boxes of other supplies 15Km from there where we are.

"We pass in review in front of the good General, who gives us a speech. The quartermaster sergeant asks me if I would cook for the General and his officers, which I do for the rest of the time that my company remains near Sailly-Saillisel. But that is not long because after a few days, we learn that we will stand in reserve in the trenches in the Little Wood in front of Maricourt, then the Trench of the Wolves in the ravine at Maurepas."

Battlefield maps show that by September 15th, Allied troops had advanced their front lines northwest of the Somme River to the Chiville and High Woods and westward to just below the small town and German-held fortress of Thiepval.

After four hard days of intense fighting and heavy casualties, what's left of Arthur company followed sub-lieutenant Peleton from the farm, back through the hospital

trench and Hauderlu Wood and onto the road that led back
to Maurepas. Not much is noted about Peleton, but from
Arthur's reference to the single silver striped rank, his "white
cord," we can presume he was a sub-lieutenant assigned to the
French cavalry. With the loss of so many officers, it would not
have been unusual for the senior ranking officer, even a sub-
lieutenant, to lead the ragtag collection of French infantrymen,
Zouaves, cavalrymen, and possibly even the occasional British
or American soldier, back to a predesignated assembly point.

In the push to advance Allied positions, Arthur's unit
was sent to secure several stands of trees, le Forest Wood,
several hundred yards east of Maurepas, with a strategic
objective of advancing on Combles's east side less than a half-
mile to the north as a prelude to retaking Sailly-Saillisel.

Leading up to Arthur's mid-September battle,
Hardecourt and its neighboring villages of Maurepas and
Guillemont had been heavily contested. Earlier that summer,
fighting had drawn to a stalemate, with the French entrenched
on the eastern outskirts of Hardecourt and the British dug
in about a quarter mile to the north. Several attempts by the
British in July had failed to dislodge German positions. It
wasn't until mid-August that French troops managed to force
the Germans to retreat down the valley back to Maurepas.
After Arthur's final battle, and for the remainder of 1916,
Hardecourt became an important support camp for the Allies,
mixing French and British troops, especially artillery. The
British used Hardecourt as a main supply depot and approach
route for long guns and troops moving up to the front lines at
Guillemont. [131]

Arthur was fighting in familiar territory, close to his
beloved du Nord in the villages about 25 miles south of Lille.
Maurepas, Hardecourt and Maricourt are about a mile apart,

---

131   "Hardecourt During WWI," http://www.chavasseferme.com/hardecourt-during-ww1.php [130]
Reuters Message, November 14, 1916

and Arthur's unit quickly skirted or traveled through them west as they passed into reserve status in the relatively safe encampments in the Little Wood and Wolfe Trench.

After "cleaning up a bit" in a new camp, it is likely that Arthur's unit received a visit of the camp's facilities by the new 32nd Corps commander, General Marie-Eugene Debeney. [132] A pass-in-review would have been expected, both as a way to visually present the camps troop strength and to introduce a new commander to his soldiers and line officers. The 32nd Corps assumed command of the section of the front lines near Sailly-Saillisel in October 1916, attacking on October 12 in a failed offensive. A second try on October 15 by the 66th Infantry Division, including two battalions of the 152nd Infantry Regiment and the 68th, a mounted infantry brigade, was more successful, capturing key outskirt positions. What followed were six days of intense street fighting, French attacks and German counter-attacks, that by the end of October left the French in possession of the village. Of the fierce attack to take Sailly-Saillisel, a Reuters Paris correspondent wrote:

> "The battle of Sailly Saillisel was resumed on Saturday afternoon. After artillery preparations, which swept away the new enemy works, the French detachments assaulted the ruins of the village. Desperate fighting ensued, the enemy offering the most vigorous resistance. Nevertheless, the fierce dash of the French crumpled up two Bavarian battalions. We retook the greater part of the village. The houses were carried one by one, each harboring one or more machine guns. At 4 o'clock the whole of the central part of the village was in our hands. The battle continued the whole of the evening and for the greater part of the night. A document found on a

---

132   "Marie-Eugene Debeney," https://www.revolvy.com/main/index.php?s=Marie-Eug%C3%A8ne%20Debeney&item_type=topic

staff officer showed that the German High Command had ordered Sailly Sallisel should be held at all costs." [133]

It wasn't that Sailly-Saillisel was key to the Allied military offensive. In most respects, it was just another knot on the rope that swung from side to side along the front. But the capture and control of Sailly-Saillisel was a morale imperative for French troops, who in August 1914 had lost the village at the outset of the war in the face of Germany's push to Paris. [134] However, reports of French Reservist soldiers, outnumbered and outgunned, killed by the Germans as they lay wounded on the battlefield were well known to the experienced French offensive forces of 1916.

CAMPAGNE 1914-1917

SAILLY-SAILLISEL (Somme). — Ruines de l'Eglise et le Cimetière.   ND. Phot.
Ruins of the church and cemetery.

---

133   Reuters Message, November 14, 1916

134   The Somme: Heroism and Horror in the First World War, Martin Gilbert, Henry Holt and Company, 2007.

(Above)   French propaganda postcard, "Campagne [France] 1914-1917, Sailly-Saillisel (Somme) - Ruins of the church and cemetery." Set 5A, DeBreteuil, Paris. Postmark: none

Sailly-Saillisel remained in Allied hands until March 1918, when it was temporarily retaken by the Germans. The Welsh 18th and 38th Divisions recaptured it again in September 1918, and it stayed an Allied asset until the end of the war. Today, a cemetery holds the remains of 771 soldiers from all of the battles for Sailly-Saillisel, brought mostly from isolated gravesites south and east of the village. [135]

---

135   Yorkshire Regiment War Graves, Sailly-Saillisel British Cemetery, France, Somme," http://www.ww1-yorkshires.org.uk/html-files/sailly-saillisel-british-cemetery.htm

Chapter Six: Combles

"I am tapped to go with my Corporal on a reconnaissance mission to Combles. We leave early in the morning. Everywhere along the road north from Maurepas, houses are demolished and the plain beyond is spotted with the corpses of French, English, and German soldiers, more Boch than the others, and a hateful odor. The Corporal and I scout Combles for 48 hours.

"When we return, someone tells us that the regiment has been assigned new orders and that we must quickly bury our dead and release the roads. It takes us all day to complete this work, and the following day we march up the line to occupy a station at the crossroads into Combles. The Boch snipe at us but their bullets are not able to reach us. They still hold the ridge above us and are able to fire a few large shells on our position. We spend the rest of the night in shell holes, then the following day we are told to relieve a section of the 1st line. We make our preparations to advance and at 1:15 in the morning a liaison officer from the frontline unit finds us and leads us to them. The site is dug into the edge of a ravine right behind a hedgerow. We have little time before daylight and immediately get to creating a workable camp. I am assigned to soup duty in the makeshift kitchen, preparing the traveling kitchens to send out to our outlying companies. This is new territory for us and we must come almost up to the entrance of Combles to find our units. We ask but nobody knows the roads. Finally, someone points down a trench that leads to the cemetery. It takes us away from the village, but we follow it anyway and when we arrive at the cemetery, we are more lost than before. Several roads lead away from the cemetery but there are no signs and no one to ask directions.

"Eventually, we reach an intersection of four roads. With our kitchens on our backs, we go to the end of each one and call for our men but in each instance, nobody answers. Finally, we blunder into the mule corral of the 1st section where the muleteers are surprised to see us. They tell us we should not have come that way; that the Boch are all in that direction. They point out the location of their kitchen, and after we transfer some of our food and fortify ourselves with some bread and drink, we must go back the same way that we had come.

147.

"*As before, we spend a lot of time fumbling around and as daylight lifts we find ourselves 20 meters from our camp but the hill between us is out in the open. It is very clear that we will have to cross the parapet in full light without cover to get to our camp. We prepare and make the dash when the Boch send a volley of shells into the field. The bombs do not reach us but we are in a poorly defendable location with no time to dig sufficient shelter. We cannot make any movement without being seen by the Boch higher up on the other side of the ravine. There's only one thing we can do: we eat soup.*"

American postcard, colorized. On back: "A French artillery division strikes a snag when maneuvering for advantageous position." (Note the downed pack animal.) Underwood & Underwood, N.Y., No. 26. Postmark: none.

Chapter Seven: Pinned down

"We spend the day pinned to the ground like this. Eventually, the Boch send some mortar shells at us, but they fly over and claim some lives in the company stationed behind us. Under the cover of darkness as evening falls, we stand up to stretch and revive our legs, then go back to finishing the trench and shelter we had started the previous day. Before we can either move forward or retreat, we will need to engage the well-defended Boch position opposite us. We send someone back to the 9th Company in the ravine behind us and are told that an attack is planned for 4 a.m. and that our artillerists have been preparing since morning to soften the open ground between us. We are ordered to take the trench and indeed at 4 a.m. some of our elements try to advance but the vicious Boch crossfire prevents it. Stopped, we miss our opportunity. The following day, we are promised that if we can take the trench, we will be relieved and sent back. In preparation, the artillery continues to bombard the Boch position all night in an attempt to demolish the barbed wire and prepare our way."

Chapter Eight: No resistance

"At 6:00 a.m. while artillerist north and south are igniting fumes and sending brass across to each other, we work to silence a Boch machine-gun hidden in the trench. It is pouring lead into the ravine. Benefitting from surprise, a couple of the bombmakers from our company skirt the ravine to reach the Boch position, jump inside, and toss a few grenades in the shelters. About fifty Fritz [sic] quickly jump out of the bunker and we take them prisoner. We pass them to the back and continue our advance, now master of the trench. Just as we pass the bunker, to the right someone is excitedly waving a small white flag. A Boch lifts his head and steps forward, followed immediately by about twenty others. They are led by an adjutant. [136] We send back word of our progress to the Colonel who then adjusts our objective that evening. We have orders now to proceed to the second trench, and we quickly advance 800 more meters without any problems or resistance. We dig into and establish a defensible position in a shell hole, secure the trench, and begin a nearly day-long effort to create a parapet where we can look down into the field in front of us. There is no resistance, so we get it done at an almost relaxed pace. Around 5:00 in the morning, five Boch planes approach to machine-gun us and drop a few bombs, but in the dark, they draw on the old trench that we quickly pushed through the day before and nobody from our Company is touched. Later in the morning, the Boch send up a machine-gun team to take away our new parapet but one of our patrols quickly jumps on them, killing a few but bringing back their gunner. Otherwise, the morning is quiet, which gives us a few minutes to move about in the open and throw a little dirt over the corpse of a Boch under-Lieutenant which has begun to stink."

---

136   *A mid-level non-commissioned officer*

Chapter Nine: Maricourt

"As dusk falls, our liaison officers leave to make contact with the command shelter to bring back new orders. The blow of artillery never stops. The liaison officers return around 9:00 a.m. with news that we will be raised and pass into reserve upon the arrival of the 1st Company. We wait expectantly for them, but they do not come. How they can get lost in a trench is a mystery, but we wait for four hours. It seems an unusual amount of time, but it does not worry us. At nightfall, the Lieutenant gives the order to leave even if we have not been relieved. A machine gunner and his rifleman stay behind while we carry all of our equipment on our backs away from the front lines in the direction of Combles. In Combles we run into our food and supply carriers who have been waiting there expectantly for us since 7:00 p.m. the day before. We transfer the material and equipment and Lt. Cordonnier gives us a few free minutes to eat and rest. Some sit on boxes, others turn them sideways to play cards. Eventually, we make our way out of Combles to the road leading south to Maricourt. Before we march into Maricourt, however, the Lieutenant insists we first inspect ourselves and then inspect each other. Then he inspects us. As smart as we can, we march into Maricourt and straight to the 165th's traveling kitchen for a cup of hot coffee. Having drunk all they had, we leave to join the rest of our regiment which is camping in a field on the north end of the Bonfray Farm. We spend the rest of the day and the following night there."

Maurepas, Hardecourt, Maricourt, and eventually Combles and Sailly-Saillisel were all contested ground in the Somme north of the river. Several battles were fought in each town during the war, although the Battle of the Somme was arguably the most devastating. These villages were reduced to rubble not for strategic reasons (the villages weren't transportation hubs, manufacturing centers, or the like), but simply because they happen to be between other points along the Front Line.

During the Battle of the Somme, the French suffered

some 204,000 casualties, the British, just less than 420,000. At first it was essentially a British campaign, with 390,000 men deployed across 13 divisions. Eventually, 1.53 million British would fight in the four-month battle. French soldiers would number about 1.44 million. [137] With such nearly equal numbers of soldiers, the disparity in casualties may be a bit surprising, but the French had fresh battle experience at Verdun and in the Somme had in-place an efficient rail system for resupplying their troops. Both surely reduced French casualty numbers to some degree.

Throughout the war, the indigenous French and invading Germans relied on heavy rail to transport troops to just beyond long-gun range of the Front lines. Then, they used portable light rail to get those men and supplies to closer staging areas. Instead of rail supply lines, however, the British Expeditionary Force preferred to use motorized lorries, buses, trucks, and cars in the Somme from July onwards. That became a problem for them. Heavy rains washed out roads and local bridges. Inadequate, overused, or poorly repaired roads were just too much for the vehicles' narrow, solid-rubber tires. Everything bogged down in the mud. At the Somme, the British artillery fired almost 28 million shells, but those shells and the nearly 20,000 tons of supplies needed to support the 12-mile offensive front couldn't always be distributed on time or where needed. [138]

Whether by truck or train, logistics required getting ammunition, food, and equipment from the larger camps like Brofay Farm to staging areas like Combles, and then to front line troops. Heavy artillery shelling meant that this couldn't easily be accomplished by trains, regardless of gauge, or cars and lorries, which needed reliable roads and an even more reliable source of petrol. Mules were often used, but by 1916

---

137   *"Battle of the Somme, (https://en.wikipedia.org/wiki/Battle_of_the_Somme)*

138   *"Transport and Supply During the First World War," Mark Whitmore, July 9, 2018. https:// www.iwm.org.uk/history/transport-and-supply-during-the-first-world-war*

they were getting hard to come by. Thus, especially for smaller items of necessity — food, water, bullets -- the last link between the maker in the factory or farm and the user in the field, ravine, or trench was a line of other men carrying backpacks, boxes and barrels.

Mailly-le-Camp was a major Allied mustering camp in the Somme. Above, "Souvenir de Mailly-le-Camp" title card, post card set, unmailed, circa 1916, C. Pinart, editor. Below "Russian troop arrival."

Above, "Mailly-le-Camp general view," N. Verry, Edition 2, circa 1916. Below, French postcard, "Malley-le-Camp. - Distribution of the Soup in camp." Both images from unmailed soldier souvenir card set.

Chapter Ten: Charles Boroyn

"On the following day we leave by car for Loeuilly, about eight miles south of Amiens. We arrive in the evening and find good people there who will put us up for the night. The next morning, I pick up again my role as cook since Guerin and I are hosted by a woman who does not know how. Besides that, though, it is a pleasant stay and after three days of rest, the regiment heads back north. I am scheduled for some leave and decide to remain in Loeuilly until the following day, the 9th, and then I take the train to Lyon.

"During my last day in Loeuilly, I meet Charles Boroyn who has just joined the regiment as a musician to reinforce our marching band. I leave with him on permission, and we travel together as far as Roanne, where we part as good friends. He leaves in one direction to visit family, and I continue on to Lyon where my brother is being treated in the Hospital Square. I spend three days with my brother, sleeping at the hospital at night and taking him out for walks in Lyon during the day. It is good to see him, and afterwards I take the train north as far as Paris, where I spend the rest of my leave."

Any soldier who has ever been in battle can describe the bonds that quickly develop between comrades in arms, the men (and today, women) who that soldier must rely on to survive, and who must return that trust. The bond can be instant and even if both lose touch through death or distance after the war, the connection is life-long and runs deep.

Arthur had such a connection with Charles Boroyn, a musician in the French infantry band. [139] Although also a trained soldier, the military musician's primary job was to stir the soup of loyalty and duty within each poilu before battle through music. Throughout his period of service, when able, Arthur visited Charles or Charles visited Arthur and after the

---

139   *No, no records give any clue to what instrument Charles played, although four drummers and/or buglers were included in every company.*

war, Arthur named his only son after his friend.

Roanne is 90km northwest of Lyon on the Loire River, about a 450-mile trip from Loeuilly, so the two men had quite a bit of a time on the train to get to know each other. In central France, both men were a long way from the front lines, closer to Switzerland and the Mediterranean Sea than the English Channel, so presumably the moments were relaxed and conversation unguarded.

If Charles had family in Roanne or simply changed trains there to head elsewhere, Arthur doesn't say. After so much time, little is known about Charles's background.

Arthur headed on to Lyon to see his brother Louis-Henry. Little is recorded about him, either. No records have been found so far to show how or where Louis-Henry was wounded, how severe, or whether or not he returned to armed duty when he recovered.

Chapter Eleven:
December 1916 to January 1917

"I set out from Paris to rejoin my regiment which by now must be out of Champagne and in the Hills of Mesnil. I get off the train at Somme – Curve into very cold weather. An orderly takes us to Camp "Allegri," which is in a ravine on the west side of the village of Saint Jean-On-Curve. While I am waiting to sign in, I take a minute to find the grave of my friend George Meurisse. I check in and get supplies and in the falling night I head out to join my company, which has advanced to the Front. I join my section in the first line trench and stand with them on watch but after a few days we change sectors and press into a part of Beauséjour. My section is part of the advanced station, but we have found a good shelter and have little to fear from German bombardments. Every day, we receive more and more reinforcements, and after eight days on the lines we are relieved by the 2nd Battalion and move back to the barracks in St-Jean.

"It has turned from bitter cold to freezing rain. It is so cold that the sweat in our boots has frozen them stiff and we can hardly put them on in the morning. Even the new bread is stone cold. We make several complaints to the landlord, but the corporal just laughs. Eventually we push through to Varionnert, but the living conditions are worse. The camp is safe from shelling but badly placed for such cold weather. We turn our tent doors away from the wind and tie down the tent fabric close to the ground to shut out the wind, but the drafts seem to come at us from everywhere. We spend the night and the following day in the tents trying to stay warm, but it is no use.

"Eventually we pull up our tent stakes and walk to Nap-Yerre where we are well received. In thanks, we help cook for and feed refugees arriving from the Ardenne. The people in Nap-Yerre remind me of home, their cleanliness and the care they take among family is like being back in Roubaix. They have little, which makes their kindness even more remarkable given that other nearby villages would rather rub salt into an open wound than share their house with us for a night. We rely greatly on

the small kindnesses of the people who agree to host us in their homes. I am not sure if these people know how much their openness means to us.

"After three days we leave Nap-Yerre to stay in Cantour, and it has even less food and shelter to offer us than Nap-Yerre. The community, however, places their intact but abandoned old houses at our disposal, so we settle in reasonably well. After a fortnight of nothing to do but try to keep warm, we leave again to engage the Huns. The Battalion must earn its pay. We remain on the relatively quiet front lines for 15 days and then leave by car for Isle-S-Ramerupt close to Areis-S-Paddle. It is my responsibility to run the kitchen for the General officers.

"Coming off of this reserve status, the regiment goes on training maneuvers at Mailly le Camp. Charles is stationed just 2km away and during this time, I visit him as often as I can. He even comes and shares supper one evening with me and the shoemaker whose home we have turned into a kitchen. The three of us cook and laugh together, the first of several nice evenings. As the cobbler interns with me to learn to cook, I learn from him to fix shoes and Charles teaches us a little music. We go together to celebrate Christmas midnight mass and attend New Year services, but on the following day, January 1, 1917, the unit departs to relieve a section of soldiers in a part of Beausejour who have not had the fortune of spending the holidays in reserve."

Arthur transitioned from the almost normal Paris city life back into life in the infantry. He rejoined his regiment 100 miles to the east of Paris in Champagne, finding them well established in deep and protected shelters. Typically, forces in the French sectors were irregularly defended, with some segments either heavily fortified or punctuated with gaps of lightly-protected and sparsely staffed ditches. In the best of cases, soldiers found themselves in deep bunkers filled with a full complement of men and equipment. Support trenches led to deeper dugouts safe from artillery shells. In ideal conditions, the No-man's land between facing armies would be hundreds of yards wide and nearly carpeted with barbed wire. On high ground, machine gunners protected well-defined entrances for patrols going "up the line" or "over the top." In the worst of cases, however, the French poilu could been assigned a shallow ditch three feet deep filled with a foot of freezing water, facing into a No-man's land only 50 yards wide. This was often a single trench, with neither a secondary line for retreat, nor perpendicular connecting supply or communication trenches. In such cases, reinforcements were forced to enter a battle from only one of two predictable directions. [140]

The British system of trenches was slightly more regular. British troops faced the enemy in a "fire trench" that zig-zagged in a pattern designed to lessen the impact of explosions and protect soldiers from flanking enemy fire. If the enemy entered the trench, a crenelated ditch, with its corners and turns, could be much more easily defended. British ditches were typically deep enough to protect from errant shrapnel, although snipers were a constant threat. Trench floors were lined with wooden duckboards and often included a "fire step" that allowed the soldier to rise above ground level to fire or charge. Unlike the French, the British usually built a second line parallel to the fire line, which they used to support logistics and stage reserve troops, but also as a fallback or regrouping area during an attack. [141]

German trenches tended to be more elaborate and better built, presumably due to the German's overall defensive strategy, which allowed units to stand and guard one place for a longer period of time. Designed to resist the concussive

---

140   *The Great War: And the Shaping of the 20th Century, Jay Winter and Blaine Baggett, Penguin Books USA, NY, NY 1996, pg. 129*

141   *ibid*

(Next page)   German propaganda postcard, circa 1915, "Zepplin over Antwerp," painted in "the style of" German Romantic artist Runftmaler Themistokles

161.

bombardments of the Allied creeping barrages [142] that preceded every attack, German bunkers ran deep. Once the shelling stopped and waves of Allied soldiers began to advance across no-mans-land, however, German machine gun crews could pop up into prepared bunkers like trapdoor spiders to annihilate advancing troops. German trench systems often came in three lines, with gaps as wide apart as 8200 feet separating their fire line (front) with the third, reserve trench. [143]

This entry in Arthur's journal marked the end of his second year as a citizen soldier. He'd started fighting at Verdun and then found himself in the Somme. He'd been shot at, bombed, and shelled. He'd starved, seen his squad decimated, and had nearly froze to death. Yet at age 22, Arthur had become an expert with a rifle, stretcher, shovel, mule, and field kitchen. Granted, the once lush forests around him were in splinters, and the once fertile farmlands were now cratered mud holes, but he'd seen much more of northern France than he ever would have imagined. Arthur had lived in tents, caves, bombed out homes, slaughterhouses, barns and greenhouses, schools, and trench craters but he'd also laughed with generals and senior officers, made new friends, earned the respect of his fellow soldiers, and expanded his skills as a cook to almost chef status.

With his even-tempered and accepting personality, Arthur was usually calm, almost fatalistic, but pragmatic, stoic, and loyal. He made friends easily in a time and place where soldiers bonded quickly and deeply for self-preservation. Again, Arthur mentions his friend, Charles. For whatever reason, Arthur and Charles clicked and stayed fast friends for the rest of their lives.

---

142   The "creeping barrage" technique sent artillery shells just beyond advancing troops during an attack. The bombardment would clear away barbed wire, machine guns, and other distractions, allowing assault troops to creep across contested ground. It involved precise and coordinated timing, however, and was more effective if charging infantrymen could tuck in right behind the exploding shells in front of them.

143   The Great War: And the Shaping of the 20th Century, Jay Winter and Blaine Baggett, pg 129

Chapter Twelve: Permission

"We unload at Valmy and settle in at Camp Firm in Dommartin-Dampierre. The Battalion can hardly contain all the troops amassed here. It has started to snow and the weather is always cold but at least in Dommartin we are assigned to sleep in hutments located a little out of town, around Somme-Bionne. In the evening of the following day, we go up the line in the left sector of Beauséjour, which is normally quiet and calm. We prepare to attack, but the Boch aggressively make their move on the line at the same time.

"I am scheduled to go on leave but the German attack forces me to stay. We prevent the Boch from advancing and ten days after calm is restored I am ordered to report to the Colonel no later than 1 a.m. It's 12:15! Not sure of my infraction, I quickly clean up and prepare my uniform. He has found a seat for me on a train making a supply run to Paris for Camp Duchaussory! I take the train leaving Nap-Peat for Elleuf where for the first time I will see my cousin Ghé. I am very well received at his place.

"I am a little sick because I caught a very bad cold in the business of these last days but Eleonor and Berthe look after me and take good care of me. I spend three days and I finish my permission in Paris where my brother comes to meet me. Like all the other permissions, it is a time to meet new friends and on this leave I make the acquaintance of Monsieurs Eugène and Maurice, who are welcoming hosts.

"I set out again from Paris to join my Battalion which is in the middle of repositioning. By late evening I catch up to the convoy, which has stopped for the night midway to Dorman. Everyone has already bedded down, so I check into the transient barracks and the next morning find my Company. They have packed up to move out, and all my equipment is stored in the trucks that follow behind us. All I can do is fall in step with the rest, carrying my suitcase. We get as far as Dormans, where we spend the night. The following day we set out again for Romaine, where all of our supplies have been sent, and set up camp in some cold, damp hollows. The temperature is brutally cold; thankfully, we spend only one night there."

It was the middle of winter and one of the first days of what promised to be another year of war when Arthur's unit hastily packed up and headed into the Marne Department yet again to relieve soldiers on the Front, this time in Beausejour. If you go looking for Beausejour on the map of France, you won't find it. It was destroyed in the battles of 1914 and 1915 and never rebuilt. At the time of Arthur's diary entry, January 1917, there was nothing left of the town, just a zig zag of trenches and deep holes from years of tit-for-tat skirmishes. Today, only a few historic markers exist where a community had thrived since the early 1800s, but in the winter of 1917-1918 it was part of the stagnant front, a no man's land of regularly tested and contested icy mud holes and barbed wire.

Ten days after their attack on the normally quiet land that once was Beausejour, German commanders had yet to follow up with a second action, providing a brief period of relative calm. Certainly, Arthur's commanding officer felt confident enough in the lull to allow Arthur to leave on permission and apparently the colonel was undistracted enough (and personally interested enough) to find Arthur a ride to Paris.

For a French soldier, Paris embodied everything he was fighting to protect: French culture, history, and a safe haven of French-centric order and sensibilities. Its normal bustle and urban chaos was a stark change to the obus exploding, machine gun sniper, adrenaline-fed terror on the Front. Throughout the war, Paris was under threat of invasion, and several times the city was within a stone's toss of the front lines, yet it remained a functioning metropolis. After the First Battle of the Marne in 1914, with German troops marching to within 50 miles of the city's gates, Paris experienced a mass exodus of civilians. Even so, 1.8 million of them remained, not including an unreported number of soldiers and temporary French and Belgium refugees from farther north. [144]

----

144   *The Great War: And the Shaping of the 20th Century, Winter & Baggett, Penguin Books USA, NY NY 1996*

Compared to peace-time standards, the Paris of 1914-1918 was gray and monotonous. The city's military governor, General Galleni, and his police force were entrusted with Paris's day-to-day security and welfare. The needy — soldier's wives, widows, orphans, and refugees — received subsidized food and fuel, both of which became critically short during the cold winters of 1916-17 and 1917-18. Municipal soup kitchens were popular. Although lines were long, the reassurance of sustenance helped maintain morale during a time where as much as 44 percent of the Parisian work force was unemployed. Coal was a premium commodity, and reserved for heat, leaving Parisians in the dark both on the street and in the home most evenings.

One exception, an unrationed luxury item, was entertainment. After the first bombs from zeppelins on August 30, 1914, Paris was initially blacked out at dusk, but as the danger receded in memory and a continued threat from the air failed to rematerialize, cinemas and theaters gradually reopened.

A soldier on permission could find much distraction in Paris in 1917. The Moulin Rouge in Montmarte was one of the first cabarets to reopen. New plays, such as the Diaghilev Ballet Russe and the shocking Ballet Parade cost just a few francs and American jazz swept the night clubs. [145] Yet Arthur reported only looking forward to visiting his friend Ghe and spending time with Elenor and Berthe, the sisters of Paul and Fernand Debryne, the two brothers with whom he had left Roubaix two and a half years before.

---

145   *The Great War: And the Shaping of the 20th Century, Winter and Baggett*

Chapter Thirteen: Tanks!

"We get under way for the 'Field of Asylum' farm where the Battalion is preparing the April 16th attack. We are billeted in barracks and underground shelters not very far from the Boch. The Company works in the woods to lay rail tracks and after eight days we return to our 'caves' to wait. I am assigned to the officers' kitchen, which we have set up in the corridor used to enter the caves. We are very well protected, although it is very cold in the caves.

"Charles's unit is assigned to the same sector as mine, and I go to see him often, and he to see me. Emile Bertran is also with us, along with two other Roubaisiens. We do not know for sure, but we all feel that the hour is close to go up to the front line. Between the four of us we have 20 francs, which we share to buy extra provisions to take with us when we go. I have made my "Pacques" with the church in Rome, knowing that for many of my comrades, unfortunately, this will be their last day.

"During the evening of April 14th, we rotate in to take our position at the Field of Asylum Farm but the sector is even more animated than I could have imagined. The Boch, who seem to know our location, bombard our hutments with shells. [146] We take refuge in some trenches close to the shelters. The following day is rather calm, although a few volleys of shells fall on us and wound some men. In the evening, the Captain leaves with the liaison officer to brief HQ about the past few day's gas attacks and he orders me to keep watch at ground level and to expect new orders soon. We move to more defendable positions, installed on higher ground in the Baumarais Wood. As we cross the road into the woods, we can see a congestion of vehicles, a great disorder of abandoned cars and lorries, many of whose remains can just be seen, sunk deep in the wet mud. For any car, the ground is impassable.

"All through the night our artillerists continue to bombard the Boch, but with their reinforced batteries, they seem to be able to counteract us at every turn. At 4 o'clock in the morning, we are ordered to halt our

---

146   *Presumably carrying chlorine gas*

advance and prepare to leave. Tanks pass us heading to the front, the first French devices that we have ever seen."

Tanks! French tanks, to be specific. Except for the obus launched by the long guns from far behind the lines, and the airplane and machine gun, up to this point in Arthur's diary, he hadn't mentioned some of the indiscriminately-brutal and mass-deadly new technologies introduced during the war. The French Army first faced German-invented flame-throwers in Verdun trenches in February 1915, for example, and Arthur must have come across them, but he never mentions it. [147] Gas was first introduced by the Germans in April 1915 but quickly adopted and refined by all sides despite an 1899 Hague Declaration forbidding its use. It was a terrorizing weapon that became progressively more brutal as the war went on – chlorine, phosgene, and then mustard. [148] It must have been in the forefront of every soldier's mind in the trenches, yet Arthur barely mentions it either. But Arthur notes his first sight of the "landships" that looked like farm watering cans, nicknamed "the tank."

Tanks had been first introduced in the Battle of the Somme by the British seven months before. The British Navy deployed 49 of them into the field during the Battle of Flers-Courcelette, at first with mixed success. As with almost any new weapon used in the field for the first time, the learning curve was steep. The tank's speed and range were limited, it was difficult to steer, and its engines often broke down, but thanks to its caterpillar tracks, the tank could quickly cut through barbed wire and bridge over narrow trenches. The tank, with its two machine guns and machine gun-resistant armor must

---

147   *"Flamethrowers," Art Patnaude, Wall Street Journal's 100 Years Legacy: The Lasting Impact of WWI, http://online.wsj.com/ww1/*

148   *"Chemical Warfare and Medical Response during WWI," Gerard J. Fitzgerald, American Journal of Public Health, April 2008, https://www.ncbi.nlm.nih.gov/pmc/articles/PMC2376985/*

have been terrifying to an infantry man who had come to terms with the flawed but comforting safety of the trench. More of a portable pillbox than an effective mobile cannon, the tank, nevertheless, proved effective enough in its first uses by the British for the French to begin to build their own. By the next spring – when Arthur reports his first sightings – the French Schneider CA had been introduced into the mix. [149]

On April 15, three newly formed groups of French tanks assembled in the Beaumarais Woods. The AS3 with 16 tanks took the lead, with AS7's 16 tanks and AS8's remaining eight tanks following behind. [150] These are likely the tanks Arthur saw. As with the British's steep learning curve months before, French tank commanders learned some hard lessons as they came upon heavy artillery barrages and shrapnel, machine gun fire, and trenches wider than they had been led to expect. No tanks from the AS3 made it back to the French lines, and only four AS7 returned. Of the eight tanks in AS8, [151] only four survived the day.

Many historians play down the impact that the tank had on the battlefields of WWI. To be sure, the weapon was deployed late in the war and only about a total of 3500 were introduced across all sides. [152] But in a war already stalemated for two years, literally entrenched in un-imaginative, carnage-producing offensive and defensive strategies, the tank pivoted

149   "Tanks," Tom Mudd, Wall Street Journal's 100 Years Legacy: The Lasting Impact of WWI, http://online.wsj.com/ww1/

150   The French Army's Tank Force and Armored Warfare in the Great War, Tim Gale, Routledge Press, 2016

151   Only eight tanks made it to the Beaumarais Wood to join AS3 and AS7. Eight broke down on the way or bogged down in the marshes along the way.

152   Germany was too slow to see the potential and impact the tank had on the battlefield. During the war, the British produced and fielded 1500 tanks; the French more than 2000. The German army, for all its emphasis on tanks in the next war, fielded just 20 machines in WWI.

battlefield doctrine. As an answer to horse-mounted cavalry and the shrapnel of the obus shell, trench warfare was introduced along the Western Front early in the war. A number of offensive and defensive weapons were fielded to offset the trench's effectiveness. But it was the tank's mobility that made the strategies of trench use and the long gun obsolete. A tank could quickly cover the contested No-man's land between enemy front lines and threaten less mobile mortars and cannons in the rear.

Of course, it is likely French Infantryman Arthur would not realize the tank's strategic impact until well after the war. To him, the noisy, smoky, seemingly-automated armored guns with his country's insignia painted on the side must have seemed like salvation-in-a- can.

Chapter Fourteen: "H" hour

"The hour H is not far off. The light cavalrymen pass us, advancing to their assigned lairs. At 7:00 in the morning we leave for our station but we only make about 2km before we suddenly come upon more congestion on the road. The front of our convoy cannot advance to the Front so we are stuck here until midday. We park ourselves in a large muddy field close to the crossroads between Poutavert and Craowel. The light cavalrymen pass by again, but this time going the other way. Several saddles are empty, In fact, the casualties seem to pass by in great numbers. We talk to men of our company returning from battle and they tell us how much we have suffered. As evening falls, we gather at our assembly area in the Beaumarais Wood where we are given orders to relieve the units on the battlefront.

"The soldiers who come off of the line are very tired and have indeed had many losses. It appears that few in the company survived. We gather the battalion and together we make for the 'Field of Asylum.' I prepare chocolate for my officers and the officer of battalion, EM. [sic.] Only one officer remains in my company: Lt. Cordonnoir is rather seriously wounded, and Lt. Courbois was killed.

"We leave in small groups; the gathering of the regiment is fixed at the exit of Vantelay in hutments. There are many breaks in the action, and we take that time to clean up a little and rest after a fashion. The next morning we set out again for Gouzacourt where we can do nothing but spend the night and begin again to march forward in the morning, each step bringing us closer to Couloumien to take a little rest."

In the previous entry, Arthur wrote that the planned day of attack would be April 16, as if it were common knowledge.

If the French poilou standing in reserve knew the attack date, unfortunately, so did the German Army. What's more, German commanders had received notice of the offensive's planned launch day in enough time to reinforce their defenses. Word had leaked out and French newspapers proceeded to

170.

advertise the whole plan. General Robert Neville, the French Commander in Chief, had personally bragged the offensive's attack date at a luncheon in London and his staff sent a written plan of the offensive to the British Foreign Office, which in turn sent it out to at least ten individuals. Even French Intelligence knew that the Germans knew of Neville's intentions. Then, as if German commanders didn't already have details and dates, during trench raids on March 3rd and April 6, they captured French soldiers carrying copies of the plan and the French Fifth Army's order of attack. [153]

Wasting no time, German commanders reinforced their nine divisions with 31 more. They added a new system of barbed wire, machine guns, trenches, and bunkers. They stockpiled ammunition and stationed troops in rear locations, ready for immediate deployment. [154]

The appointed "hour H" was indeed April 16. Later referred to as the Battle of Chemin des Dames (Ladies Way), the Allies 5th and 6th Armies attacked along a 40km front between Soissons and Reims. Predictably, they stepped into a meat grinder.

Even under days of Allied advance heavy artillery fire to soften the way, German fortifications remained intact. From Craonne to Cerny-en-Lainnois between April 17 and 22th, the French could make no headway and the offensive failed. It cost the French nearly 140,000 casualties. [155] On April 23, British forces launched a second wave to provide cover for a French retreat, costing the Allies an additional 150,000 casualties. [156]

153   In Flanders Fields, Leon Wolff, Time Reading Program, Special Edition, Time Incorporated, NY, Pg. 81

154   ibid, pg. 83

155   Le Chemin Des Dames, http://www.cheminsdememoire.gouv.fr/en/le-chemin-des-dames

156   An Overview of the Nivelle Offensive," Michael Fassbender, http://michaeltfassbender.com/nonfiction/the-world-wars/battles-and-campaigns/an-overview-of-the-nivelle-offensive-1917/

At the end of nearly a month of fighting, whatever appeared as gained ground to Allied commanders was actually part of a calculated German retreat strategy set months before to straighten out a hard-to-defend bulge in the Front, a fallback position called The Hindenburg Line.

Incidentally, Arthur mentions Gouzeaucourt, a small village in the Nord that had been overrun early and spent most of the war under occupation. It was destroyed by the Germans during their retreat in early 1917 and by the time Arthur's regiment and the rest of the Allies arrived, it was "found empty, a mass of smothering ruins." [157] The reason Arthur's unit could "do nothing but spend the night" is because there was nothing left of the village. [158]

To Arthur and to most French infantrymen after Craonne, the war must have seemed hopelessly locked up, each day bringing the same exhausting routine: fight, retreat; fight, rest; stand ready in reserve, advance to the front. Live, get wounded, or die. Eat, clean up a little, starve a little, sleep in the mud. Walk, cook, eat. Wait. Soldiers in the trenches had to all be asking the same question: "When will it change?"

The defeat at Craonne and the Battle of Chemin des Dames, begun with such enthusiasm, hope, and bravado, was devastating to French morale. The weariness in Arthur's tone as he writes reflects his sinking sense of frustration as the regiment's losses mounted and he saw how brutally the villages and countryside in his beloved Nord have been ravaged by the Germans.

---

157   *Quote from Capt. H. FitzM Sacke, M.C.,"Gouzeaucourt during WWI," http://www. worcesterandgouzeacourt.org/home/index.php/wwi-and-gouzeaucourt/49-wwi-and-gouzeaucourt*

158   *Later that year, the Allies attempted to push past Gouzeaucourt and through the Hindenburg Line using tanks for the first time as an integrated element of their battle strategy but without a follow-up plan to hold their gains, they were forced to fall back in early 1918.*

Detail, American propaganda postcard, "French Moving on the Enemy's Flank," Underwood &
Underwood, N.Y., No.25. Image from card postmarked Antigo, WI, July 15, 1917

PART FIVE:
AFTER CRAONNE, APRIL, 1917 to
BASTILLE DAY, 1918

"Now it is your turn, all you big shots,
to climb the ridge, because if it is war you want,
pay for it with your own skin."

-- *"Song of Craonne," ballad, lyricist anonymous [159]*

Prominent in the battlefield where Arthur's regiment was gathering north of the Aisne River was a road that topped the crest of a plateau. The road predates the 1700s but was paved in 1780, as the story goes, in order for the daughters of King Louis XV to visit one of their ladies-in-waiting. The road and the plateau became known as the Chemin des Dames. [160] The road was punctuated by two bastions on either end, Mount Laffaux, with its ancient mill, the moulin de Laffaux, to the west, and the plateau de Craonne to the east.

The Craonne plateau rises to as much as 130 meters above the surrounding Ailette and Aisne river valleys, its sides steep and craggy. French troops looking up at German positions would have to had wondered what their superiors were thinking. The plan to conquer the plateau required the French infantrymen to cross another 7-12 miles of valleys and ridges and secure the open plain surrounding another hill leading up to the small city of Laon. Surprise was not an option. Even if German commanders didn't have advance information about

---

159   *"France Commemorates Dark Time in History," Rick Smith, April 2017, NY Times, http:// www.nytimes.com/2007/04/15/world/europe/15iht-mutiny.4.5296462.html*

160   *"The Nivelle Offensive and the Battle of the Aisne 1917," Andrew Uffindell, Pen & Sword Books, Ltd., Yorkshire, England, 2015*

the attack, due to the size of the amassing French army and the elevation of German troops atop the Chemin des Dames, every move and pre-positioning could be observed by the plateau's defenders. To complicate matters, the weather was uncooperative and German aviators controlled the skies above the ridges, making Allied reconnaissance nearly impossible, especially of German units and activities on the plateau's far side.

For the French, entrenched and committed to a policy of offensive warfare at any cost, the battle was a bloody defeat. The battle for Craonne, also called the Battle of the Chemin des Dames by French historians, and simply referred to as "the Nievelle Offensive" by the British, cost the French 40,000 soldiers on just the first day. French medical services were unprepared for such numbers and soon became completely overwhelmed. While such high casualty numbers were not necessarily disproportionate to other WWI offensives, internal soldier and external public perception fueled by war-weariness and impatience by 1917 labeled the battle a disaster. French Commander in Chief Robert Nievelle found himself relieved of his commander-in-chief duties and reassigned to oversee France's battles in Africa a month later.

Discipline broke down on an unprecedented scale among soldiers who had witnessed wave after wave of fruitless and mass-deadly attempts to capture the high ground. Possibly bolstered by news of a Russian people's rebellion farther east, thousands of French soldiers revolted, staging demonstrations and refusing to advance. Government and military leaders publicly classified the short-lived uprising as a series of small, independent mutinies but even soldiers who did not take part felt the despair in the air and sympathized with the cause.

After three years of war, it is not surprising that inside the French Army was a pressure cooker about to blow its valve. The differences in life style and authority between officers and the lower ranks, especially when it came to privileges and pay, were wide and obvious. Court marshals for commissioned officers were "not infrequent occurrences," [161] but punishment for an offense was most often temporary confinement to quarters (dismissal not being an option in wartime, of course). For non-commissioned officers and the rank-and file infantrymen, however, even small infractions had larger consequences. Punishment was severe and considered a frequent necessity in France's compulsory army, an institution made up of men from every social class. [162] Reductions in rank were rare, but a French soldier might be confined to barracks or imprisoned for very minor offenses. [163] An infantryman might expect punishment in the form of extra guard duty or additional tasks in the ordinary or inspection while on parade carrying a full complement of gear. For criminal or repeated offenses, a soldier could be confined in prison or transferred to one of the Algerian disciplinary battalions, the French Foreign Legion. [164] Punishment was something that happened so regularly that it was almost a part of the normal, expected routine in the life and career of the common soldier.

In late April 1917, most French soldiers would have fresh memories of heavy casualties in Le Esparges, the slaughter in the Somme, and then Craonne. At a time when reading a newspaper in the barracks constituted an offense of discipline, the political and strategic military reasons for such mass losses as discussed in the papers were hidden from the average soldiers unless they happened to catch up with the news while on permission. Imagine how a conscripted infantryman would have felt after reading in a newspaper smuggled into the barracks and hidden from his superiors, that his Russian equal in the trenches

161   *The French Army, pg. 39*

162   *The French Army, pg 42*

163   *British counterparts might receive either a reprimand or reduction in rank for the same offense.*

164   *The French Army, pg 41*

of the Eastern Front had rebelled against what would seem to be similar senseless slaughter.

Arthur's diary provides some clues to attitude changes in the wind. He describes a French public that is beginning to withdraw its in-situ support of French troops serving in reserve status. And creeping into the tone of Arthur's writing is a sense of despair and questioning. It's possible that this could be attributed to Craonne as the cause, but it's just as likely that Craonne was a symptom of a malaise that began with the Russian Revolution or maybe even earlier, at Verdun, perhaps, or as a result of the disastrous first days of the Battle of the Somme.

Public support and sentiment for victory at any cost waivered when casualty reports became known after Craonne but the French government could not afford to show weakness in its resolve to win the war. Neither the enemy nor the French people could be allowed to see a breakdown in the rigid authority afforded France's military commanders so, while there was acknowledgment of the legitimacy of the poilus' complaints, the discord was labeled as isolated mutinies, not a revolution, and quickly dealt with by military tribunal. It is thought that refusals to carry out orders occurred in about 68 of France's 110 divisions. Finding the instigators turned out to be difficult, however, but none-the-less, French war councils handed down about 3600 convictions. In many cases, a quota of soldiers was chosen by lot and arrested as representatives for their unit. Typical sentences ranged from "right of grace" pardons, to forced labor, or lengthy imprisonment. Five hundred and fifty-four men, however, were reportedly sentenced to death for their parts in the uprising, and possibly as many as 70 were actually executed by firing squad. [165]

---

165   *The actual numbers are in dispute. Just after the war, the French Government officially reported executions in a range of 60-70, although some sources at the time put the range from between 49-55. Recent historians, however, argue the actual number could be as low as 30.*

Detail, French postcard, "Inside the Infantrymen's Kitchen." Aqua Photo, Paris. Postmark: none

It was a quiet turning point in French military culture. If the losses at the Battle for Craonne had any silver lining at all, perhaps it was that the new French military leadership, led by Verdun's hero General Henri-Philippe Petain, made sweeping changes in France's military doctrine of offensive warfare. Petain overhauled and re-choreographed the army's approaches to tactics, training, and equipment. He addressed leave and pay and inequities and restructured the organization of the French Army, making it into a more efficient and lean fighting machine. Furthermore, Petain ceased offensive engagements until France and Britain's newest ally, the Americans, could reinvigorate the Western Front with fresh, new troops. [166]

---

166   *"The Nivelle Offensive and the Battle of the Aisne 1917," Andrew Uffindell, Pen & Sword Books, Ltd., Yorkshire, England, 2015*

Chapter One:
Rubber, coal, and cotton

"We leave Gouzacourt to retire and recover in Romilli, not very far from Dorwan. I remember this because we all get dysentery from some rather bad cooking, The people who were supposed to be our patriotic hosts were either crazy or angry and almost refused even to let to us sleep on the old straw left by the soldiers who left before us. I am not sure what those men did in Romilli but thankfully, when we recover, we leave for Chatillon. Here the community does support us and we cook and eat among good, very clean people, and as grateful to host us as we are thankful to be hosted by them. We divide up and dine in the evening among several local families. It would have been nice to stay longer but the next morning we are back on the road headed for Plessier, a very small country community, where, although they have very little, they nevertheless hosted us well, too. Always following someones planned schedule, we leave Plessiers for Houdevillers, where we catch up with the battalion. The first night we join the 3rd Battalion and cook together but after that I am assigned to the officers' kitchen, where I cook for the 3rd's commander and his staff. Those of us assigned to the officers are relatively well off, with a good bed and regular meals, two things we have not had often in the field and two things we do not take for granted."

-- April 21, 1917

Arthur's entry is dated April 21st, but let's roll the calendar back a few weeks to the beginning of April 1917. Although Arthur did not know it, things actually had begun to change for the better ten days before the April 16 attack on the Fields of Asylum farm. On April 6, the United States of America officially aligned with Britain, France, and Russia, eventually committing two million American soldiers, sailors, and airmen to the war.

As important as this reinforcement of fighting men was to the Allies, U.S. participation also meant an influx of raw material and a revitalization of supply lines for much needed manufactured equipment, goods, and food. By 1917, after two and a half years of war, France's mining, farming, and manufacturing industries were exhausted. Before the war, France was producing 41 million tons of coal annually. [167] However, now many of France's coal mines were situated in the northeast providences on the German side of the Front. [168] Access to raw materials, such as coal for fuel and copper for shell casing, are considered strategic centers of gravity in any modern war, and like a gyroscope wildly wobbling, this French center of gravity was dangerously close to imminent collapse. With the exception of coal and rubber from France's colonies, nearly all the raw material needed to sustain a war had to come from France's allies and from overseas purchases. A year later, records show that France was importing and consuming 6,276,000 metric quintaux [169] of petroleum, 2,539,150 metric quintaux of cotton, 451.850 tons of nitrate, 265,788 tons of copper, 18,310,000 tons of coal, and 148,600 metric quintaux of rubber. [170] It is no coincidence: the influx of such goods and material can be attributed to the direct contributions of machines and material from and supply lines strengthened by the United States' entry as an ally.

From his limited ground-level perspective in the trenches, however, Arthur and his fellow soldiers would not have known or noticed that the tide of supplies and equipment was now rising and Germany's relative strength to wage war was ebbing.

---

167   *The French War Machine, Shelby Cullom Davis, Unwin Bros, ltd, 1937, pg. 164*

168   *The French War Machine, Shelby Cullom Davis, Unwin Bros, ltd, 1937, pg. 163*

169   *An old unit of measurement of mass (symbol q) equal to 100 kilograms*

170   *The French War Machine, pg. 163*

Chapter Two:
Endows and Baune

"*We spend five good days there, then we are sent to Endows, close to Coulommiers, a small but beautiful and very clean town where the inhabitants are very nice. We set up our Company kitchen in an uninhabited house. The owners live elsewhere in town and have given us permission to occupy only the bottom floor but we cannot resist laying down in real beds, although either the Lady of the house does not notice that we are sleeping upstairs or has chosen to ignore it.*

"*Charles, whose unit is assigned to Rebais, drops by to see me when his Regiment band comes to put on a concert for the town. The Colonel and several other officers organize a hunt to flush out wild pigs in the nearby forest but only succeed in killing a small number. Regardless, every day we have game to cook (pheasant, wild rabbit, or hare), and I make several trips by bicycle to Coulommiers to get cheese and provisions.*

"*My friend Fernand Castelain also drops by to say hello. His unit is stationed in Montmirail. And my friend Jacques, too. I receive a letter from my brother and it says that Madeleine has returned to Paris. That certainly makes me smile: she will have news and letters from my dear parents. I immediately put in a request to take some compassionate leave.*

"*After ten nice days resting in Endows, we head to Mount-Dolphin for the night. We set out the following day for Toult but nobody in that town wants to put us up. Instead, we find the nearest military unit, requisitioning meals from their kitchen and camping nearby. It is unusual that we were not received well by the locals, but we make do with what we have and pass the time. We leave the following morning for Baune, where I set up the Company kitchen in a cheese factory.*

"*While in Baune, my request for three days leave is granted and I travel by train to see Madeleine in Paris. Unfortunately, I arrive in the city at 4 o'clock in the morning on a Sunday, but I cannot wait so I immediately take the subway to Vincennes. I wake up my brother and Madeline but spend three wonderful days with them. They do bring news from home, and I am happy and relieved to know that everyone is safe and in good health.*"

From the first time that a clan of cavemen put out sentries to guard against the encroachment or attack from another family group, the acts of surveillance and sentry duty have involved brief moments of physical action and adrenalin, punctuated with much longer stretches of waiting, boring housekeeping chores, and even rest.

The daily routine for French poilu was similar. Life in the trenches started about a half-hour before sunrise with a call to muster, or "stand to." The whole platoon assembled fully armed and ready just in case of a dawn attack. On a calm day, sentries were assigned and posted and the rest of the men had breakfast. Next might follow an equipment inspection, another sentry rotation, trench maintenance, dinner, and a change of sentries again in the evening. Sniper fire or aero attacks occasionally broke the monotony, but otherwise on such days, it was a boring, lice- and often rat-infested, mud-or-dust existence. [171]

Life in reserve status included many of the same duties – mustering, cooking, equipment inspections and maintenance – but at a slightly more relaxed pace. Being billeted in a nearby village often meant warmer and dryer living conditions, either because the soldiers were put up in the spare bedrooms of villagers whose own sons were fighting elsewhere, or because they were allowed to occupy houses vacated by refugees. Soldiers might have time to hunt rabbit or wild pigs in local forests or fields, or bicycle to town or explore the countryside. It was the task of commissioned and non-commissioned officers to keep their soldiers out of trouble and in the good graces of their hosts and the local constabulary. To foster good community relations, soldiers often volunteered or were assigned to assist with refugee services, farm chores, or menial hospital duties. If, like Charles, they played an instrument in one of the French Army's regiment or battalion marching bands, they

---

171   *The Great War and the Shaping of the 20th Century, Jay Winter and Blaine Baggett, Penguin Books USA, NY NY, 1996, pg. 132*

performed at daytime events such as ceremonies and funerals or presented evening concerts.

Except for compassionate leaves to attend to family emergencies, "permission" days off were only allowed when a unit was in reserve status.

French postcard, "A French Machine Gun," by L.V.C, Series A, No.4. Postmarked Territoire de Belfort [a department in eastern France].

184.

Chapter Three: June and July, 1917

"I leave Paris and rejoin the regiment at Maurenbert (near Paddle in the Aube department), where they are practicing maneuvers at Mailly-le-Camp. I must travel several times into the local villages to get supplies for the officers. The country is sparse and rural, and although there is little to do for recreation, we have a rather good stay.

"The regiment leaves for Fountain-Loeuillière, arriving on June 15th. We prepare a good meal, expecting the officers to eat when they arrive, but they leave immediately for an evening in Troyes. We wait dinner on them for nine and a half hours, but they do not return so we eat and start packing up our equipment. The regiment must leave by midnight. We sit around for about an hour on the grass next to our packed cars and lorries, but at midnight less than a quarter of our officers have returned. Out of time, the Company assembles and we move out to join the regiment at the rendezvous point in Savière.

"In Saviere, we are warmly welcomed at a large farm, where the owner gives us each a bottle of 'puit to eau-de-vie' that has survived the shelling. Having eaten nothing but some coffee since leaving Fountain-Loeuilliere, it is not long before every bottle has been opened and we are feeling the warming effect of its alcohol. A little challenged for balance, we march off into the night and arrive on June 17th at Ossey-les-Trois-Maisons. We've traveled back and forth through France but this is new country for us, where they do a lot of knitting by machine.

"Remarkably, these people continue to work and manage to be happy. Once I have finished cooking for the officers, the rest of us dine with the families in their home. At one point, there are 18 of us around one table, including several young ladies, and we have a lot of fun. We spend two nights there sleeping in a good bed, then it is back to Longfertes where we spend one night.

"The next day we march on to Saint-Brice, which is close to Provins, headquarters for the General of the regiment. I am scheduled to take some leave, so on the 22nd, I head out to explore the countryside for

seven days. I rejoin the regiment in Provins a week later. I enjoy the rest of our time at Saint-Brice, taking the opportunity when I can to go into Provins, where Charles is stationed. Our company remains in Saint-Brice until the morning of July 9th, when we head north through Lougeuville, eventually unloading in Bergue and setting up camp in Nieppe. We stay in Nieppe until July 16th."

Before the war, infantry officers marched with their infantry soldiers. It demonstrated to the world that in France's egalitarian culture, when it came to danger, the officer shared the same risks on the battlefield and was as personally invested in a battle's outcome as the poilu. By the Spring of 1917, however, the officer-enlisted gap had widened. From Arthur's reports, at the very least, the officers appeared to be eating and sleeping better than the enlisted troops.

Uncharacteristically, in Arthur's mid-June diary entry, he reported an indulgence on the part of his officers. They had apparently abandoned the regiment, or at least left it in the hands of its senior non-commissioned officers, to essentially eat and run upon arrival at Fountain-Loeuilliere. Why? Apparently to spend an evening in Troyes. Wholesale, the officer corps apparently left for town. It would be as if a unit's officers were tempted with rare tickets to attend their favorite rock concert. Arthur describes how the unit almost missed deploying on time because the officers "had a late night." It is possible that his observation and the way he recorded it in his journal reflects a slight change in his own attitude towards authority and possibly the war, perhaps a symptom of or a fallout from the April mutinies after Craonne.

Troyes was a quaint medieval town of 55,000 citizens just before the start of the war, but an industrial center. Some sections still sported cobbled streets lined with half-timbered houses that date back to the 16th century but other areas hosted modern factories that produced textiles, hosiery, and knitwear. [172]

---

172   *Troyes, https://www.britannica.com/place/Troyes*

Several famous Gothic churches graced its skyline, including the Troyes Catherdral, the Eglise Sainte-Madeline, and the Saint Urbain Basillica. The latest opera, Helen of Troy, may have been in town and since these were the days before radio and television, the more educated officer caste may have climbed over themselves to get front row seats. But it's more likely that going to church or seeing the opera were the last things on the officers' minds. Troyes, like 34 other towns and cities in Northern France, was home to some of the French Army's official brothels. One such place in Troyes today, the prestigious La Mignardise restaurant at 1 Ruelle des Chats, is rumored to have been a brothel at one time. [173] Comfort houses, called "les maisons tolerees," that sported red lights were for enlisted troops, where a soldier might meet a girl, spend his money, and be out in time to have supper with his buddies in one of the local taverns. Brothels for officers, identified by their blue lights, were often plush, sometimes opulent establishments, offering meals, drinks, entertainment, and an entire night's stay.

After a hundred years and no one to ask, it is hard to tell whether Arthur's reproachful tone reflected a sour attitude towards some of his officers, an irritation that they let the food he had carefully prepared go cold, or whether it was simply meant to communicate his distaste for such carnal recreation.

In any case, even with orders to move out that day, the kitchen stayed open and ready for the officers for nine and a half hours, then closed up just in time to disembark by midnight. Presumably, Arthur and his unit had been told where they were heading: unlike some entries in his diary, he doesn't write that they were marching off into an unknown future. No, Arthur presumably knew he was heading north into familiar territory: Flanders and the villages and cities along the French and Belgium border.

---

173   "Meeting with Didier," *Troyes Couleurs On-line, https://troyescouleurs.wordpress. com/2017/06/10/rencontre-avec-didier-defontaine/*

French postcard. unmailed, inscription reads "*When, in the assault, one rushes, one goes there, without hesitation. At the slightest resistance, a salvo of kisses!*"

The closer they got to Bruges, just a few miles from the Belgian border, the more excited Arthur must have become. These were familiar roads, ones he would have crossed several times a year as a civilian in what probably seemed a lifetime ago. He would have bicycled off to Bergue twice a year to pick up supplies for his butcher shop. In Nieppe, a few miles from Lille, he would have traveled occasionally for spices that came into the town from boats on the Leie River.

Arthur would have seen the destruction left by the Germans retreating to the Hindenburg Line, their scorched earth policy removing anything of value and destroying anything that the French and British might strategically use against the Central Powers, be it a well-standing building, bridge, or rail depot. But Arthur was to stay in his beloved Nord less than a week before his regiment moved into Belgium to support as yet another offensive, this time the Third Battle of Ypres.

Chapter Four: Belgique

"On July 16th, 1917 we leave by car along the main road to Bergues, headed for the Westinleterey monastery in Belgium. We assemble not very far from the new front lines which the Company patrols for four days. I remain in the rear with the support team and every evening I assemble the traveling kitchen and send supplies to the officers at the front. After four days we are called up out of the trenches and sent back to Quadypre in France, where we camp for eight days. I spend several of those days resting among the dunes at Dunkirk, but eventually we reassemble and set out again, this time to Rexpoode. While the Company goes to the Front, I remain with the supply depot in Westinleterey. It takes us three days, but we advance to our objective, Baroque 58, which is on the main road between Furnes and Yprès. We man the line for 14 days, and then stand down for 47 days in Bambecque, 15 km from Bergues on the Belgium border. During my days there, I often walk the beaches off Malo and take several bicycle strolls in Dunkirk.

"While in Bambeque, some of the Battalion travels south for three days of artillery and rifle training in St Pol. On October 7th we head up into Belgium and prepare to attack on October 9th. My Company is assigned to defend positions in Wood 16. I work with the kitchens supporting the 2nd Battalion's line along the Yser.

"We are raised on October 16 and return to Warher. We are always kept in the vicinity of Bergue. The food is terrible, almost unpalatable, but I am not the cook. I do not suffer from it much anyway because I soon leave on permission. I depart the Front at Bergue for Elleuf, where I spend three days with Téo, who receives me well, and then return to Paris to pass the rest of my permission."

The French marked it as the Second Battle of Flanders. The British military called it the Third Battle of Ypres; the Germans, Flandernschlacht. The British media and historians would refer to it as the Battle of Passchendaele. By whichever name, the offensive to reestablish an Allied presence in Belgium ran from July 11, 1917, until November 10, as both the Allies and the Central Powers attempted to take or hold the ridges south and east of the Belgian city of Ypres in West Flanders.

Arthur's unit left France on July 16, 1917 for the first time since the war began, stepping into the trenches and coastal fields along Belgium's southern border with France. A combined force of French First Army and Belgian troops defended the Yser Front, a 19-mile stretch of swamp along the Yser River between Nieupoort and Westende. The Belgian Army had defended this northern-most segment of the Western Front since their victory against an invading German Army in the first Battle of Yser in 1914. Just across the river from German-occupied Dixmude, it was an important segment of the Front to hold yet because the swampland could neither be crossed with large equipment nor easily captured by advancing troops, it was of little strategic concern to German commanders. Thus, it remained a relatively quiet area for most of the war.

The same could not be said of lowlands just a few miles south, where the Yres bent north to the sea and the Yres Canal and its support road ran south to Ypres. In late 1917, six divisions of the French First Army and 18 divisions of the British Fifth Army defended this ground, which had turned into deep, sticky mud after years of fierce defensive and offensive fighting.

It was Arthur's task to organize the traveling kitchen and food supply runs from the monastery at Westinleterey to both the Belgian troops defending the Yser Front and the British fighting to secure the flank between Belgian and British frontline positions. While the British were organizing to advance towards Ypres, Arthur's unit was assigned to hold the main road connecting the village of Veurne, just two miles from the coast. To this end, they dug in.

After the mutinies in the French Army earlier in the year, Allied commanders believed it prudent to let someone other than France lead the next major offensive, especially if it promised high casualties. Since the Americans were not yet on the scene, it fell to the British again to take the point.

The Third Battle of Ypres began on July 31st 1917 with an attack by the British on Passchendaele, about ten miles to the south. Situated on the eastern-most ridge outside of Ypres, Passchendaele could serve as an important staging location for troops and aircraft. From Passchendaele, the British and French could launch attacks on a critical German 4th Army railway junction at Roulers, potentially strangling German supply lines along the northern front lines.

For Arthur, this offensive would have been especially personal, with Passendale just 20 miles from his hometown of Roubaix, and the last portion of Belgium not under Germany's control. Arthur mentioned preparing "to attack on October 9th," and that his company had been assigned to defend French positions in "Wood 16," presumably in the Houthhulst Forest along the northern flank of the salient.

In what became known as the Battle of Poelcappelle, October 9th opened with French First Army and British Second and Fifth army attacks along a 7.7 mile stretch of the front in Flanders from just south of Broodseinde to Saint Jansbeek. This was the fourth push in quick succession, with the first three -- the battles at Menin Road Ridge, Polygon Ridge, and Brodseinde – having methodically achieved their objectives. The goal for October 9 was to get halfway to Passchendaele but heavy rain and a strong German counter offensive slowed down the advance. In the end, the Allies could not hold the ground and the initiative failed.

Just as in the Somme a year earlier, this was essentially a sector of the Western Front assigned to the British Expeditionary Forces and just as in the Somme, the Third Battle of Ypres was initially designed to take pressure off of French forces fighting to the south. At the cost of 310,000 British casualties and 260,000 German soldiers, [174] on November

6 Canadian and British troops captured their main objective, the village of Passchendaele, 10 kilometers miles from Ypres. The casualty toll to the Allies was so staggering, however, that the British commander, Sir Douglas Haig, declared the battle a victory after Passchendaele and decided to halt any further advances.

Chapter Five: On the Yser Front

*"I leave Paris to come to find the Regiment with the camp of
Metz-native, close to Rousbruge. The Company is helping build the
hospital at Waayenburg, an English station. We leave the camp on
November 14 to stand the line and I take my post in line II B in a
Belgian shelter. It is well built and dry. It is my task to make soup every
evening for the officers and deliver it with a traveling kitchen.*

*"At the beginning of December, the English are able to relieve
us. They arrive just in time to silence the Boch batteries, our own heavy
artillery having recently retreated, leaving a void that sprinkled unanswered
shells on us. But not anymore. Everywhere, it seems, the English install
their own batteries and pillboxes and it is not long before they control the
situation."*

The Third Battle of Ypres had been won but two weeks
before, with "won" used to describe at least a temporary quiet
in the trenches.

The region known as Flanders stretches about 150
miles from just east of Dunkirk almost to today's border with
Germany. On the west, it encompasses the coastal ports of
Zeebrugge and Ostend, occupied by Germany throughout
WWI as access points for submarines and light naval surface
ships to the North Sea. In the middle are the near-coastal city
of Bruges and Belgium's capital, Brussels, and the port town of
Antwerp on the River Scheldt.

Where the Western Front passed through West Flanders
in late 1917, the land is mostly flat, so flat that even a small hill
tens of feet high was considered a strategic prize. Like Kansas
in the United States, perhaps, or the flatlands of Hungary, the
terrain offers few natural landmarks. Mount Kemmel, 350 feet
high, drains some of the area's rainfall, but rivers and canals
wind seemingly at random to or away from the sea around long-

ago sand dunes and now-exposed river deposits of fine-grained clay. Because of its mild gradient to the sea, during the rainy seasons the area's shallow waterways cannot discharge enough water. The surrounding lands flood into swamps and boggy islands. [175]

Unlike the Somme, the soil in West Flanders fields is clay mixed with water. Clay plus water equals mud but not the chalky mud of the Somme that Arthur and his comrades were used to, but the gooey, smelly mud of primordial swamp slip.

Field reports in the archives of the British War Office about the Yser's notorious mud include comments such as "Part of company bogged in communication trench south of St. Eloi; two men smothered," and "Trenches full of liquid mud. Smelt horribly. Full of dead Frenchmen too bad to touch. Men quite nauseated." The soiled landscape of decaying bodies and war debris sank into the mud and was slowly washed out into the black water of canals and ditches. Such conditions were most severe on the sea-side of the Yser River where the land is lower than sea level at high tide. [176]

Unlike the Somme, neither the Allies nor the German Army could dig trenches, which would have almost immediately filled with water. Instead, German soldiers built up concrete pillboxes, sometimes three feet thick, which served as high ground, shelter from bombardment, and a solid foundation for small artillery and machine guns. The Allies, with their offensive philosophy, at first constructed less temporary wooden bunkers, but as they advanced and the German Army retreated, the French and British quickly moved into and commanded the concrete pillboxes.

From October to December, 1917, Arthur was assigned to support the Allies General Headquarters and the Belgian

---

175   *In Flanders Fields, Leon Wolff, Time Reading Program Special Edition, 1958, pg. 120*

176   *ibid, pg. 123*

Army in and around Nieupoort. It was the Allies northwestern-most section of the Western Front, stretching from Arras in France north to the sea. Returning from leave, Arthur caught up with his regiment at Metz, near Roesbrugge. Roesbrugge, now called Roesbrugge-Haringe, was located a mile and half from the French border, about a mile west of the British hospital camp set up on the grounds of the Chateau of Vlamertinghe in Waayenburg. Like everything else in the area, the terrain is lowland, drained by small streams and canals that flow into the Yser, then the North Sea. With seasonal rains and the heavy traffic of men, horses, and equipment, the roads and upturned pastures would have been an impassible sea of mud had it not been for an extensive Allied network of plank roads and duckboard tracks.

The Third Battle of Ypres was officially over by mid-November. The British had accomplished their pre-battle objectives by the first of the month and Arthur's unit had moved in to hold that ground. Then British and Canadian forces moved on to capture Passchendaele, a small village to Ypres's north. They succeeded, and as before, Arthur's unit was moved into place to hold the line but that assignment didn't last long: a German offensive was brewing farther south and soon French infantrymen in Flanders found themselves in a double time march to counter it.

Chapter Six: Back to the Somme

"On December 5th, 1917, the smoke clears and we can take a breath and relax a little. We come into Woesten to spend the night. People have come out of their basements and the town seems to be getting a little more animated since our recent advance. We are supposed to embark with Crombeque for Loon-Plage but we cannot find to place to camp in the field so we are installed in the village of Ropenaefort along the Channel. Compared to the past month, we are not badly placed, but we only spend four days there before we leave on foot for Lillers.

"We arrive on December 9th in Burbure, close to Lillers, a caravan of automobiles and trucks follows the Battalion carrying our tents and tarps and the surplus of equipment which the men cannot carry.

"We find good people to put us up and we set up station in Marquay, not far from St.-Pol-sur-Ternoise. After settling in, I leave to get provisions for the kitchen and get as far as Roellecourt when I meet Louis Deschamps who was with us in Verdun. I am so happy to see that he is safe. Upon my return to Marquay, we set up a kitchen in a large farm house for one night, leaving the next day to spend the night in Sericourt, close to Frevent.

"It has become very cold and now it starts to rain. In Sericourt, we are billeted in a smart little villa with a good bed and the following day -- as with every day now it seems -- we take up another stage of our march. We leave Sericourt for Le Souich where we attempt to set up in their school, but it is too badly damaged. The roof leaks and the wind passes through the walls as if they are not even there. After one miserable day of rest we head to Vavignie the next day, where we spend the night, only to set out again for Bretel, not far from Doullens, the day after that. The cold weather has turned freezing and it begins to snow. We are placed in a hay barn, but the lady living there whom we have befriended by helping her cook insists that we not sleep in the barn. Instead, she lays down mattresses and blankets on the kitchen floor next to the fireplace. We play nain jeune [177] after supper with

---

177   *"Nain Jeune," or "Yellow Dwarf," a 19th Century traditional French children's game based on a cartoon character of the same name, combines cards, tokens, and playing board in a parlor game of luck and calculation.*

the farmer and his family, and afterwards we lie down for the night, thankful for the heat.

"In the morning, we muster to march out. The temperature is very cold and deep snow has fallen overnight, making it very difficult to walk. We do not get far, convening for the night in Bertangles. I am paired with an old chef to cook for my comrades, and the gentleman passes on to me some wonderful advice and wisdom.

"It snows and snows, so much so that the roads are covered. We head out by foot hoping to cut through Amiens to reach Camon before nightfall, only to find that the road is boxed in, buried in snow drifts as deep as 80 cm in places. The road has become a bottleneck of stalled trucks, and we are forced to pull them out of the drifts and back onto the road. The company marches to the front of the stalled convoy -- more than 20 km of immobilized cars and trucks — and then marches in front of it in two rows to pack down the snow. In this way, we climb up and down the hills in advance of our supplies while the others manage to follow after a fashion. Eventually, the Regiment arrives in Amiens, where we are received as heroes, the crowds there acclaim our miraculous arrival through the snow and throw us cigarettes and delicacies."

When Arthur almost casually mentions that he can "take a breath and relax a little," it's neither a figurative statement or hyperbole. The battle for Ypres had been brutal, with soldiers fighting under clouds of burning mustard gas lobbed across No-man's land by German artillery. British forces had captured Passchendaele by November 6 and the Battle of Ypres ended four days later, but at great cost in both casualties and loss of life. [178] By mid-November, 1917, twelve divisions from the British Second and Fifth Armies and French 1st Army, including Arthur's, had completed a four month-long offensive to push back German defensive positions north and east away from the hills and ridges around Ypres. It was a questionable, qualified victory, with almost no

---

178   "Battles: The Third Battle of Ypres, firstworldwar.com, http://www.firstworldwar.com/ battles/ypres3.htm

land gains in some areas of the Front and a maximum of three miles in others.

While the Allies settled into their new defensive positions in Belgium in November and December, however, fighting began to heat up yet again along the Somme River in France. In the relative quiet after the Battle of Ypres, soldiers may very well have felt like they could relax but, unfortunately November 20 marked the start of the Battle of Cambrai. Ten days later, with the advent of a German counterattack, Arthur and his comrades would be needed elsewhere, and needed quickly.

Winter arrived early in December 1917 and it stayed for what seemed like forever for the soldiers stuck in trenches or marching to new battlements along the Front. If the soldiers in the trenches and tents up and down the front lines on both sides thought the Winter of 1916-17 was brutal, they were in for a terrible surprise. The winter between December 1917 and March 1918, the fourth of the war, was to be the harshest of any winter during the conflict. [179]

By the beginning of 1918, a fully-staffed division of 12,000 men was supported by about 1,000 tons of supplies every day, even more in an offensive operation where supplies had to be stockpiled and ready to move forward with the advance. [180] Wherever the fight broke out, men, machines, mobile hospitals, and supplies had to be moved, regardless of the time of year, the temperature, or the weather.

---

179   *Invasion 14, by Maxence van der Meersch.*

180   *"Transport and Supply During the First World War," Mark Whitmore, July 9, 2018. https://www.iwm.org.uk/history/transport-and-supply-during-the-first-world-war*

Chapter Seven:
Chateaus and castles

"We arrive at Camon on the East bank of the River Somme outside Amiens. I set up to cook for the company in a kitchen of an old woman who is a little crazy but she lets us bed down in her living room, me on the settee and the others on mattresses. After a good night's rest, we are back on our way to Jumel where we are to regroup. We still cook and sleep among good people who take effort to make our stay pleasant. On the 22nd we leave for Bonneuil. The roads are always encumbered of snow and the weather makes traveling very difficult. The horses suffer much.

"Because the roads are bad, it takes us until December 23 to get to Essuiles Saint-Rimault. We arrive in Agnetz on Christmas Eve and are placed in the castle of Mr. Cuvinot, senator of Oise. He puts the castle completely at our disposal. To prepare the midnight Christmas supper, I go into Clermont to get provisions. The temperature is criminal! When I get back, we prepare the midnight meal, and then retire in the pre-dawn hours in warm beds thanks to the good folk here who agreed to rent us a room. We stand down Christmas day, but we leave in the morning of the 26th for Laigneville, which is close to Creil. We stay in Laigneville through the 27th waiting to confirm that we will have a place to stay at our destination and when the arrangements are complete, we spend the next day traveling to Mont-l'Eveque, four kilometers out of Senlis.

It has taken us 23 days to walk here, nearly 150 kilometers on foot and in the snow. The men are happy to finally be able to rest longer than the few hours of sleep we have stolen along the way. I set up the company mess in the incredible castle of Mr. Montalba, cooking on the same furnaces used to prepare food for the masters. The stable staff puts their horses at our disposal, the servants treat us as royal guests, and the chambermaids provide us clean, comfortable beds. We sleep very well. I help as best as I can to prepare the traditional New Year's Eve midnight supper, but I leave early on permission for Paris to spend two days with my brother and Madeleine.

"When I return, I make several trips to the market in Senlis with the chef of the castle and the head waiter, who I have come to know and respect. We are often visited by Mr. and Mrs. De Montalba, our kind and gracious host and hostess. Then, on January 5th, the company leaves for Verneuil to help instruct new machine gunners of the C.I.II [sic]. In Verneuil, I am assigned a room over a busy tavern and although our quarters are much smaller than the incredible accommodations at Chateau de Montleveque, we cannot complain. The owners provide us a comfortable room and I help wait tables to pass the time in the evenings.

"Except for one day of leave in Paris with my brother (Madeleine having left to maternity), I help train in Verneuil for about 15 days. The new recruits will make good soldiers and our hosts are good, kind people who appreciate what we are doing for them. On January 16, we return to Mont-l'Eveque where we rejoin the rest of our regiment and prepare to depart the following day. We are headed in the direction of Ceri-Manival, which used to be in beautiful country but now the countryside has been severely damaged by the Boch. They have mined a large part of the village, since we did not give them time to destroy it. We set up after a fashion in Ceri-Manival and spend the night, only to set out again the following day for Dampleu. We are assigned to occupy an area that the Germans have been forced to evacuate, systematically destroying everything in their path. They saw the trees, demolish the mines, poison the wells, and raze every building down to its cellar.

"All the country which we cross is evacuated and we request of Bon Dieu that our poor Nord has not succumbed the same fate under three years of invasion. A sad show, we pass what is left of Saint-Pierre-Aigle on the 19th and cross Bucy on the 20th. We camp near Bucy for a few days waiting for orders, then advance towards to Celles-sur-Aisne, where we are billeted in wine cellars. Stone racks do not make comfortable beds. The Company takes this time to complete a few tasks we have had to put off, such as equipment repairs, and work on the shelters to improve them as best we can."

It was early December 1917 and Arthur's unit was redeploying. From Camon, just east of Amien, they were to head south down the Noye River through Jumel to Biennial les Eaux, a journey of about 25 miles. They were heading towards Creil, where they were to help train and qualify the latest wave of new infantrymen on machine gun tactics.

Having slogged from Camon through heavy snow, the terrible storm forced Arthur's company to spend one night in the twin hamlets of Saint Rimault and Essuiles, reaching Agnetz the day before Christmas. Agnetz was a picturesque community on the edge of the Forest Domaniale de Hez-Froidmont, about 40 miles from the Front at that time. It was a relatively quiet town in Oise, a department of France about 50 miles from Paris. Arthur's unit, with its marching troops and a convoy of trucks and horse-drawn wagons, arrived in near-blizzard conditions. The elements of the convey were split up for the night, with most of the officers and horses billeted in the Chateau de Agnetz, which the owner, Oise senator Cuvinot, had given over to the Army as a bunkhouse of sorts for troops recovering from front line battle. The rest of the soldiers were parceled out to whomever could take them in, both in the town and the surrounding villages. As his unit's cook, it fell to Arthur to prepare the soldier's Christmas Eve meal, traditionally a festive respite from normal rations. So as to accommodate the large number of soldiers, the meal likely was hosted in the Chateau de Agnetz's Great Hall.

Arthur braved the deplorable temperature and heavy snow drifts on a road of questionable safety, traveling by motor lorry to the nearby village of Clermont to get provisions from the Army commissary. Returning with sufficient food, presumably he served his unit a satisfying meal. With kitchen clean-up afterwards, it would have been very late, possibly early Christmas morning, before Arthur retired to a rented bed elsewhere in the town, hosted by some family looking forward to their own Christmas morning meal.

(Next page)   _Detail from "Bringing in their Wounded Corporal," scene from Arras, U. S. post card, W.C.A., Series 146, unmailed._

Bringing in their Wounded Corporal.

© BY UNDERWOOD & UNDERWOOD, N.Y.

On December 26, the storm passed and the company attempted to leave. They got only as far as Laigneville, about seven or eight miles down the road, before stopping for the day, either because some roads were still impassible, or to meet up with other units, or both.

To their great surprise and pleasure, upon their arrival in Mont-l'Eveque, the company was hosted at the Chateau de Mont-l'Eveque, a fairy tale castle if ever there was one. Even grander than the Chateau Agnetz, the gothic Mont-l'Eveque, with its four slate-roofed, flag-topped corner towers and stone-balustered catwalks would have been impressive.

Arthur writes of his concerns for his hometown, Roubaix, and the du North department where he grew up. His concern was well founded. During the ravaging winter of 1917-1918, the wool textile industry city of Lille and its cotton textile towns of Roubaix and Tourcoing, as well as other communities in du Nord and in Belgium – Valenciennes, Anzin, Cambrai, Maubeuge, and Bethune -- were now German-occupied territory. Even if there was little direct fighting, the residents would have continually heard the guns firing on both sides of the front, no more than 20 miles away. The barrage became a fact of life for almost all of the war, with the Front never varying more than a mile or two. [181]

Although textile work all but shut down, Lille became strategically important to the Germans precisely because of its proximity to the Front. At first, a railhead and spur were built in Lille to supply the front lines, but soon a network of rails connected Lille to Valenciennes, and from Valenciennes it ran to Charleville-Mezieres and Bale, but also north to Brussels, Liege, Cologne, the Ruhr and eventually Rhineland. [182]

But with practically all able-bodied French and German males now serving in uniform, building this rail network fell to

---

181   As described in French-Flemish writer Maxence van der Meersch 1935 novel Invasion 14, translated by W. Brian Newsome, McGill-Queen's University Press, Montreal, 2016.

182   French and Germans, Germans and French, Richard Cobb, University Press of New England, Hanover, London, 1983, pg. 4

forced labor groups made up mostly of boys and girls sixteen to eighteen years old from Lille, Roubaix, and Tourcoing. Pressgangs, the feared and hated Feldgendarmerie, nicknamed the "diables verts ("green devils" for their tall, green collars), would raid neighborhoods street by street at night with packs of Alsatian hounds. Any of-age child rounded up in their net would be bonded into forced labor for six months or longer, some to build the rail system, but others to lay out barbed wire and field telephone lines, dig deep gun emplacements and ammunition dumps, or harvest crops in the Ardennes fields of southern Belgium, Luxembourg, and Germany. [183]

In an attempt to limit civilian movement and communication, the occupying German forces imposed strict curfews, required passes for anyone crossing into different quarters of their city, and restricted travel between towns. Even funeral convoys required an armed escort. [184] Public buildings and upscale private homes were requisitioned for officer housing and soldier barracks. Every civilian was required to salute every German soldier they might pass in the street. Some roads were closed or restricted to all but German personnel and rationing was introduced.

Predictably, rationing immediately led to the creation of a black market and a loose resistance to German occupation sprouted up as early as 1914 in Lille and Roubaix, with heroic acts reportedly carried out by wine merchants, school teachers, and mill owners. A priest is recorded to have set up a clandestine transmitter in Lille and in one instance, locals helped Allied agents in Roubaix escape to Holland. Some resisters were caught and publicly executed in the Citadel in Lille, but many were not [185] and lauded as heroes after the war.

---

183   *French and Germans, Germans and French, Richard Cobb, University Press of New England, Hanover, London, 1983, pg. 6*

184   *ibid, pg. 25-26*

185   *French and Germans, Germans and French, Richard Cobb, University Press of New England, Hanover, London, 1983, pg. 25-26*

Chapter Eight:
February to May, 1918

"*I am scheduled for permission. I leave Ceri-Sermoise for Elbeuf where I spend three days with my cousin Théo Maryns, who receives me very well. While passing through Rouen, I am able to say hello and catch up with Celine, a friend from Rue Charlemagne. [186] It makes me quite happy to hear and be able to speak a little Roubaix with her. From Rouen, I take the train to Paris where I spend the rest of my leave like so many others, far from my parents and my dear Roubaix. I am with friends and my brother but it is not the same thing.*

"*On February 16th, 1918, I return to the Front. I find my Company at Jlennes in the Aisne near Craonne. My Uncle Henri is stationed in the same village with his pigeon soldiers, and they often come to tell me hello (and to taste my cooking). We remain in this place until March 22nd, when we leave for Maizy. We are placed in new hutments around the village, and from these barracks each day the Company goes to work. It is a relatively safe place, well back from the Front, and the Boch spare us their artillery, although we are occasionally visited by aero planes that throw bombs around to change the landscape.*

"*We leave Maizy for Roucy in the Aisne Department, a country which is not new to us. We have already had occasion to spend several lifetimes here. Not having their own kitchen and mess hall, my officers eat with the staff. I stand down for eight days. With no place to go, I spend most of my off time in the canteen. We remain in Roucy until the 30th and deploy for two days to Revillon to prepare again for another long march. On the 3rd we are in Bazoches-sur-Vesles; the 4th in Arcy; and on the 5th and 6th we find ourselves in the ruins of Cartiers to take a little rest. On the road we meet a lot of convoys in retreat, folding up and moving back under the German capture of Soissons.*

"*The Boch are advancing and we are massing to counter them. I run into my Uncle Auguste and together a little later we visit Uncle Henri who is*

---

186   *Possibly the very Celine Arthur wrote a letter to but never mailed on his first day of the war.*

camped in a tent next to his pigeon loft, tending a portable lamp to keep the birds warm. We move out on a forced march to Pont-St.-Pond where we are put up in formidable structures where even the large artillery shells cannot penetrate. The Boch can draw on us but we do not fear anything. In the evening, we support an attack by the 11th Infantry on Chateau de Coucy: two sections take positions in bushes at the edge of the bluff overlooking the chateau, making a crossfire of machine-guns. At night, we shelter in the caves of Pont-St.-Mard.

"We share the parapet with the artillery officers who regulate the shelling across parts of a forest road that we can barely see in the distance. We can make out what appears to be a Boch pillbox which the artillery officers tell us shelters one of the German long cannons that can draw on Paris. We are there for eight days, after which we leave for Sorny where we stay until the 13th. Everywhere we go it is the same: desolation and ruin.

"By the 14th we are in Venizel, protecting a flying division. They need our support. This is an animated sector, one without a clear objective and it is hard to anticipate German intentions. They seem to initiate skirmishes everywhere. On the 19th we move out again, this time to Ressons-le-Long, where we stay one night. In the morning of the 20th, we depart for Rethondes, a small community near Compiegne. But we are very badly received there: the village is very small and its inhabitants would rather we just go away. After four days imposing ourselves on the villagers (without incidents), we march off to St. Leger Woods in Compiegne. The woods are beautiful, not just because we are used to seeing the forest in splinters or miles of rolling farm land. The Company erects new British hutments and we settle in nicely. We cook for some of the local gendarme, hoping to profit from some of their news but also to keep our men in their good graces. Corporal Mauselin goes in search of fresh mushrooms, and several times we hunt for game in the woods to put fresh meat in the larder. All in all, a very pleasant stay."

Perhaps French Intelligence reported a massing of German artillery, a sure sign of an impending offensive, or perhaps it was a change in logistics traffic, refocused in the Ainse region at the expense of other German outposts along the Front.

Whatever precipitated the redeployment, in early February Arthur's company mobilized and Arthur, returning from a few days leave, caught up with them in Jlennes. He remained there until March 22.

As the French First Army combined divisions along this part of the Front, it would not have been unusual for Arthur to run into or serve with friends and family. Since divisions and regiments were organized geographically, it was the rule rather than the exception for men from the same towns, regions, and departments to serve in the same or sister units. Arthur wrote that during his redeployments at this time he briefly ran into Uncle Henry-Edmond, brother of Arthur's father, and Uncle Auguste, his mother's brother. Nothing is recorded further of Auguste, but Henry, it seems, served as a pigeon soldier in the Signal Corps.

For reliable, short distance communication across the battlefield, nothing rivaled the pigeon in WWI (and in fact during WWII). Du Nord in particular was and still is renowned for its love of pigeons and pigeon racing and the skills of the birds' handlers. [187] Unlike copper telephone wire that could be easily cut, the carrier pigeon, outfitted with a small message-carrying metal vial tied to one of its legs, was difficult to shoot down. More than 100,000 of them were used during the war, with an astonishing message delivery rate of 95 percent. [188] Birds would be carried to the Front lines in baskets strapped to a soldier's back. A communications specialist would then write, load, and launch intelligence or battlefield updates, sending them literally "on the wing" back to wagon-based coops parked tens of

---

187   *At the outset of the war, Germany ordered French civilians to destroy their pigeons to disrupt communications between the French and British armies. The price for non-compliance: execution. A statue dedicated to the carrier pigeon's role in WWI was erected in Lille, France, in 1936. (http://www.remembrancetrails-northernfrance.com/trails/the-war-of-movement-and-the-first-german-occupation/monument-to-carrier-pigeons-lille.html)*

188   *"Pigeons and WWI," The History Learning Site, https://www.historylearningsite.co.uk/world-war-one/the-western-front-in-world-war-one/animals-in-world-war-one/pigeons-and-world-war-one/*

miles behind the lines tended by soldiers like Uncle Henry. You might say it was the early 20th Century's version of "wireless communications."

History records that the German Army launched the first of four spring offensives, Operation Michael, on March 21, suggesting that Arthur's unit's move from Jlennes to Maizy was an attempt to stem the German advance. But the German Army crossed the Front lines into Allied-held territories at Arras, more than 100 miles north of Maizy. Operation Michael eventually bogged down for logistical reasons after advancing south to within 10 miles of Amiens, about 70 miles from Paris.

In late March and in early April, Arthur and his fellow soldiers marched back and forth through Roucy, Revillon, Bazoches-sur-Vesles; Arcy; and the ruins of Cartier. About five miles separates each of these villages, a clear indication that the French Army suspected an imminent second attack but had little precise information about where a new offensive's vanguard might attempt to push through.

On April 9, the German Army initiated the second phase of their spring "Kaiserschlacht," or "Emperor's Battle," this time successfully punching a hole through the front at Lys, Belgium, in Flanders, about 50 miles even further north of Arras, close to where Arthur had been fighting three months before. At the cost of heavy casualties, Allied forces fought back this offensive in Bethune, which German commanders titled "Operation Georgette," all but destroying the city's center. [189]

By the end of April both the Kaiserschlacht's Michael and Georgette operations had run their courses but anticipating a third offensive, French commanders had Arthur's unit protecting the countryside in the Aisne south of the Oise River. Arthur writes that his company helped the 11th Infantry

189   "*Kaiserschlacht: The German Spring Offensive of 1918,*" *http://www.remembrancetrails-northernfrance.com/history/battles/kaiserschlacht-the-german-spring-offensive-of-1918.html*

storm what was left of the Chateau de Coucy, [190] marking them in Coucy on or around April 24. From high ground about two miles away, Arthur shared a top-down view of the chateau, helping the artillery observation crew spot and report on the location of German pillboxes, machine gun nests, and heavy artillery.

Nervous about a flanking move from the east into Paris, it is obvious that French commanders kept Arthur's company mobile: Sorny, Venizel, Ressons-le-Long, and Rethondes, a small community just east of Compiegne. In Rethondes, a strategic crossroad across the Aisne, the villagers' mood was clear: they didn't know who would occupy their town in the coming days and they preferred not to be contested ground. Apparently, they made such a row of it that Arthur's company crossed north through the Foret Domaniale de Laigue to the small community of Saint Leger Woods and established a camp in the cover nearby.

Saint-Leger-aux-Bois was a small village along the south bank of the Oise River, just above where the Oise and the Aisne rivers merge. Surprisingly, it still exists, despite heavy fighting between Allied and Central Power forces that started sporadically in the Spring of 1918 and carried on into August and September in what became known as the Second Battle of the Somme.

Once in place in the Saint Leger Woods, Arthur's unit wasted no time establishing a comfortable – and presumably fortified – base of operation. They surely erected a canteen and mess hall (where they hosted local law enforcement), tents, and a new British invention, the nissen barracks.

Unlike the rough, wooden structures Arthur and his comrades bedded under during training, at Verdun, and in the

---

190   *The German Army blew up much of the 13th Century castle's four towers during their March 1917 retreat.*

less-than-field conditions at more established camps and depots earlier in the war, by late 1917 and early 1918, many Allied soldiers in reserve status and established camps were assigned a relatively dry bed in a nissen hutment, the original quasit hut. The British version of the hutment was invented by American-born British Captain Peter Norman Nissen in early 1916, then a mining engineer with the 103rd Field Company of Royal Engineers. The nissen, as it came to be known, was a portable, factory-built structure that could be packed in a standard military wagon, unloaded in pieces, and erected or disassembled by six men in four hours. Three prefabricated 10' corrugated iron sheets were bolted together and bent in an arch spanning either 16, 24, or 30 feet. Each span was held rigid by attached purlins and straining wires, and each purlin in turn was bolted to anchor plates on the ground. Spans could be overlapped and attached together to create almost any length. Wood and weatherboard walls plugged the half-cylinder shelter on each end, with windows and doors framed in to provide not only entry, but light and ventilation. It is estimated that more than 100,000 nissen hutments were produced during the war. [191]

But Arthur's unit didn't stay long enough in the Saint Leger Woods to enjoy the accommodations: in less than a week, they were on the move again.

---

191   *Nissen Hut, https://en.wikipedia.org/wiki/Nissen_hut*

Lieutenant-Colonel Peter Nissen standing in front of a Nissen Hut talking to a British Sgt. Major in Blangy, France, in April 1916. In the doorway of the hut stands a guardsman of the Welsh Guards. Image courtesy of National Library of Scotland.

Chapter Nine: Through the Oise

"On May 1st, 1918 we leave for Jonquières through the Compiegne Forest, which we cross. Compiegne is too large for our division to defend and military engineers keep the bridges mined and ready to blow up in case we are forced to jump to someplace else in the event of a German advance. We walk six more kilometers, skirting just north of Compiegne to arrive at Jonquière. We stay with a fish farmer, who is worried about his fish, but we persuade him that it is impossible for the Boches to advance that far. The next morning we take the road to Lancourt in Oise, returning to a very beautiful country untouched by the war, where there are many castles. It is like coming home.

"We stay in the villa of a former shoe-maker, an Austrian from Francourt who has been imprisoned. Compared to some places we have stayed, we are treated like royally here, but not for long, unfortunately just for the one day. The following day brings a complete change of scenery: we are hosted at a farm that does their best to receive us despite being destitute. We try to leave them with good memories. Then on May 5th, we march to within six kilometers of Bauvais, stopping in a very pretty but small rural community where the inhabitants all make buttons and brushes from bone and antlers. We are close enough to travel into Bauvais for supplies and we walk around impressed. It is an old place and the capital of the Oise department. It is quite a change to find ourselves so near a big city, having become accustomed to always being quartered in small villages that usually do not have more than a couple hundred inhabitants, including in that count the many men who are off fighting the war someplace else.

"We are fortunate to be able to spend 15 restful days among the good people in and around Beauvais, who help us forget for awhile the harder moments of the war, and who provide us with such quarterings."

Leaving the relatively quiet St. Leger Woods, Arthur's company headed southwest to reinforce French forces protecting Paris's north flank as the Germans initiated two consecutive offenses, the Second Battle of the Somme in

March and the Battle of the Lys in April. For French and Allied commanders focused on planning their own offensive, the Spring and Summer of 1918 required flexible strategies and logistics, not to mention accurate intelligence and reliable communications. Troops were repositioned like foils in a fencing match. To the infantrymen, it was a time of rapid movements, then long periods of watching and waiting.

Ironically, or perhaps prophetically, Arthur's unit traveled through the Compiegne Forest towards Jonquiere, on their way to Bauvais. Six months and eleven days after Arthur's diary entry, the Armistice was signed in these woods.

Beauvais was then and is still today a major city in France. Arthur would have been impressed with its gothic La Cathedral du Saint-Pierre and meandering Le Therain River, presumably having preserved its charm (and cathedral) by having the good fortune to be further south and west of what became the German offensive salient.

Early in the Spring of 1918, the German Army attacked British Fifth Army positions along the Somme River at Saint-Quentin. It was the first major German offensive in more than a year and it started with a saturation of shells from more than 9,000 artillery pieces. Initially, the German goal was to move north to seize Allied supply ports on the English Channel but after two very successful days on the attack, commanders changed their plan. Instead, they pushed west, moving 72 divisions 40 miles past the British defensive units to within 80 miles of Paris before their logistics and supply network began to stretch too far and break down under heavy French resistance. German commanders had hoped to split French and British forces, but for the first time, American units of significant size joined French and British troops in the trenches, helping to tip the momentum in the Allies favor. By April 4 it was clear that the German Army advance had stalled.

Then, like a deadly game of whack-a-mole, the

German 4th and 6th Armies pushed against British positions at Armentieres in northern France in the Flanders region on the River Lys. Their goal was nothing less than to force the British out of Belgium, to push them back to the coastal ports in France and relieve pressure on the submarine ports in Zeebrugge and Bruges. German commanders focused their forces on a 10-mile front along the river, starting first with a four-and-a-half hour-long bombardment, followed by some 2000 tons of poisonous mustard and phosgene gas. But after the surprise in the Somme a month before, this time British troops were better prepared and limited the German Army's advance to about ten miles.

It was not unreasonable to expect a third German attack in as many months, so in mid-May it is safe to say that Allied preparations, as well as the troops and support units they commanded, were in a constant state of movement and readiness. As it turned out, the German Army attacked one last time that summer, this time at the Chemin des Dames ridge along the Aisne River in what was to be called the Third Battle of the Ainse.

Chapter Ten: To the Aisne

"It is Monday morning, May 20th, 1918. We travel around like a band of gypsies. We spend the night with Nivelle's Calvary, and although there are already too many troops in one place, we find some high ground to bed down temporarily. The best thing we can say for it is that it keeps us out from under the wheels of the passing trucks. Fortunately, the following day we find a place in the High Spine, where at least there is a breeze. We wait, expecting orders. When they come, they do not contain details but 27 cars bring us back to the St. Leger Woods where we wait through the afternoon and the night. Early the next morning, we take over a ravine near Jaulzy and spend the night.

"While we have been gone, the Germans have been busy. They must have advanced on the heights of Tartiers because we can see in the distance that the airfield we guarded is in flames. On the following day, we leave without the mules, all of our equipment on our backs, into the Coeurres Wood. Despite some shade, everything seems to glow in the terrible heat. We arrive by evening and begin to prepare to spend the night but we receive orders to proceed to the front in Ambleny. When we get there, my group takes its position in the fortifications but I stay in Courtanson to arrange for mules and manage the kitchens, and to serve as liaison officer to the Company. I spend much of what remains of the day and overnight at the Company headquarters in Ableny but around 11:00 a.m. we quickly pack up and with haste move south. I stay with the combat train, but it is as if we are caught up in the chaos of a stampede, with orders, then counter-orders, all the while Boch planes sniping at us with their machine-guns.

"We finally establish a camp near Puisieux, where we remain for four or five days, then receive orders to leave for Mortefontaine where trucks and cars will take us to new positions along the line in Mareuil-s-Ourcq. It is now June 5th, and the appointed time for our sector. We go up over the trench top opposite Ferte-Milon, which has been bombarded into mud holes. Most of what is left of any house or shed foundation is just a pile of loose stone. We take one trench.

"The artillery and our exploration of abandoned trenches are but preparations for a great offensive planned for July 17th. We hold our ground for six days, then step down in reserve, regrouping in Auteuil. Several times in my duties as cook and kitchen deliverer I cross Ferte-Milon and shake my head at the disaster it has become. It was a beautiful town once. The festival of July 14th comes and goes without incident or ceremony, with all our thoughts, conversations, and focus on the counter-offensive. A day or two before, the artillery starts to arrive. The H-hour is rumored to be moved to the morning of the 18th but nothing is quite certain so we wait. It has rained all night, a terrible storm, washing away the footing under much of the artillery, yet they continue to fire. Judging from the rate, the bombardment on the Germans must be terrible. With the break of day comes a break in the rain. It is now 5 a.m."

The regiment headed out of Beauvais, having rested for a couple of weeks in or near the city. They made their way south through the Oise Department, skirting the Somme for about 40 miles into the woods and valleys around Compiegne. Compiegne guards the confluence of the Oise and Aisne rivers, with the Oise draining the woods and farm lands from the north and the Aisne traveling from the eastern planes and hills. The delta where the two rivers merge was canopied forest, the Foret Domaniale de Laigue, with its more ancient St. Leger Woods further up-river on the Oise's eastern bank. Arthur's motorcade of cars and trucks crossed the Oise River, presumably at one of the smaller villages of ancient Roman origin – Longueil-Annel, Janville, or Thourotte -- and made camp for the night in the Saint Leger, about three miles northeast of Compiegne.

The regiment had been here before. Germany had lost this area in the Second Battle of the Aisne during the Nivelle Offensive, which had been so costly to the French that it led to the mutinies of 1917 in the French Army ranks. A year later, in May 1918, it fell to the commander of France's Sixth Army, General Denis Auguste Duchene, and to British Lieutenant

General Sir Alexander Hamilton-Gordon of the British 9th Corps, to defend the Aisne. Four divisions of Hamilton-Gordon's army had just posted on the relatively quiet Chemin des Dames Ridge to rest and regroup.

Arthur's entry starts on May 20. His unit was moving around like a wrestler sizing up an opponent in the ring. Eventually, his company took up position in Jaulzy, on the south bank of the Aisne River. On May 27, the German Army initiated a major surprise offensive, called the Third Battle of the Aisne by the Allies or in German history books, Blucher-Yorck, in the area of the Chemin des Dames, about 40 miles away.

The timing is worth noting. Arthur records his unit's rapid redeployment from Belgium to the Ainse River a week before the German Army kicked off its offensive. Clearly, the French had developed better surveillance or had credible intelligence of an imminent attack.

Nevertheless, when it came, the German Army demolished four French divisions and advanced their front lines 12 miles in six hours. They captured Craonne and raced to the Aisne River. Two days later, the French city of Soissons fell, and the British and French each lost four more divisions trying to plug the breach. [192] By May 31, the German Army had established a 35 miles deep salient stretching to the Marne River, capturing both Chateau-Thierry and Dormans. The Marne is a tributary of the Seine River which runs through Paris, and Paris was just 35 more miles away.

Arthur records a series of movements orchestrated in quick succession: the Coeurres Wood, Ambleny, Puisieux-en-Retz, Mortefontaine, Mareuil-sur-Ourcq, and Ferte-Milon. In the span of about eight days, his company moved 20 miles southeast along the front, then west about ten miles, and then

192   "1918: Third Battle of the Aisne begins," This Day in History, History Channel on-line (https://www.history.com/this-day-in-history/third-battle-of-the-aisne-begins)

south about 25 miles to Mareuil-sur-Ourcq. They finally engaged German troops on June 5th, about five miles north in La Ferte-Milon. Arthur recorded the incident as a relatively minor skirmish ("we take one trench"), and soon afterwards his 110th regiment began to dig in at La Ferte-Milon to prepare for a major offensive planned for mid-July.

German commanders hoped Blucher-Yorck would force the Allies to move their forces around and take some pressure off of Allied attacks on troops in Flanders, which was potentially threatening important submarine ports in Belgium. If Arthur's diary is any indication, that goal for the offensive worked well. Germany's strategy, too, was to capture as much territory as possible before the Americans could establish themselves in northern France. But on the battlefield, by the very end of June the first United States troops had arrived in Italy; the Allies had kicked off the Battle of Le Hamel in the Somme; began an offensive in Albania; and still managed to initiate the Second Battle of the Marne, designed to push Germany out of Chateau-Thierry. Much to German commanders' dismay, the American tide had already begun to rise.

Although Bastille Day came and went without incident for Arthur in the trenches, actually July 1918 was a signature month for the Allies, both on the battlefield and strategically elsewhere in world events.

Away from the front in France, not that it made much difference except symbolically, July 1918 brought both Haiti and Honduras into the war on the side of the Allies. July marked Germany's last attempt in WWI to use airplanes to bomb the British Isles and Field-Marshal Conrad von Hotzendorff, the author of Germany's siege strategy of Verdun, was relieved from duty as commander-in-chief of its Austro-Hungarian armies. Sultan Mohammed V of Turkey died that month, to be succeeded by a more moderate Mohammed VI.

In December the year before, Russia had declared a ceasefire with Germany, essentially opting out of the war, but if there was even a glimmer of hope that they might further assist the Allies, [193] it would have been dashed to the ground with the July execution of Tsar Nicholas and his family. Yet Russian resistance to German occupation continued to prevent a redeployment of German forces to France: Germany's ambassador was murdered in Moscow on July 6, the French joined with what was left of the North Russia Expeditionary Force in Murmansk on July 26th, and Field-Marshal von Eichhorn, commander of the German Army in the Ukraine, was assassinated in Kiev on July 30th. [194]

By July 15, 1918, the Western Front ran from the North Sea down to just east of Allied-held Ypres, south in a line down to French-defended Amiens on the Somme River, and east to German-occupied Soissons on the Aisne. From there, the German salient bulged south through Chateau-Thierry across the Marne in France's Champagne region, then ran due east to Verdun and the Meuse River. Beyond the Meuse, the German Army held the Woevre Plain and pushed on more than 150 miles of France's departments south of the Lorraine all the way to Switzerland. For an invading Germany exhausted by nearly four years of stalemate in France, with military units fighting in Turkey, middle Europe, Italy, North Africa, and on open oceans across the world, the Third Battle of the Ainse was a bold expansion, but unsustainable.

If July showed stress cracks in Germany's brightly painted metal well bucket, the holes that rusted through from the inside in August and September eventually drained it dry of options and led to talks of a cease fire in October.

---

193   *There wasn't.*

194   *"The Great War Timeline -1918," http://www.greatwar.co.uk/timeline/ww1-events-1918.htm*

PART SIX:
ENDINGS AND BEGINNINGS

A number of factors from 1917 carried over and began a confluence that led to the end of the war in 1918, although few could have predicted the consequences of such events at the time.

In March 1917, Germany began to draw the center of the Western Front northwards and consolidate their troops along what they called the Siegfried Line, or what the Allies referred to as the Hindenburg Line. By eliminating a contested bulge, German logisticians could eliminate the need to defend 25 additional miles. Details of a Russian Revolution reached soldiers along the Western Front in the Spring of 1917, including news that masses of Russian soldiers had mutinied and joined the revolt. In April, the United States declared war on the Central Axis, coming into the conflict on the side of France, Great Britain and Russia.

This good news, as mentioned, was offset by the failure of the French 5th and 6th Armies to break through the new German Siegfried Line in a conflict that became known as the Nivelle Offensive, after the architect of the attack, French Commander-in-Chief Robert Nivelle. The French failed with staggering casualties, precipitating the Craonne mutinies by French poilu in the trenches and leading to disheartening but effective summary executions by French leaders to quell the revolt.

In late June, the first American soldiers began to arrive, taking positions along the Front. The Russian Army lost a major offensive to recapture Lemb in July, and regardless of Allied pressure on the Axis divisions along the Belgian border in the battles of Ypres that summer, Germany's pressure on the Eastern Front, along with their support of Russian dissidents

221.

Vlaimir Lenin and Leon Trotsky, wore down Russian resistance. That fall, after Lenin's October Revolution, Russia pulled out of the war, freeing 44 German divisions to head westward to France. [195]

On the surface, the outcome of the war for the Allies seemed bleak but the underlying truth told another story.

Although the Siegfried Line allowed Germany to densify their troops and equipment, it was a sign of a larger strategic weakness. Germany was beginning to feel their losses, from attrition, certainly, but also from naval blockades that began to dry up the flow of natural resources and supplies to feed the war machine. French and Russian troop mutinies shook both Allied and Central Axis commanders to their core, for without confidence in their basic, most fluid and expendable tactical tool, their soldiers, commanders could not have confidence – actual or perceived – in their own strategies. [196] The Americans, although raw on the battlefield, learned quickly from the experienced British and French and their enthusiasm, equipment, and numbers of men more than made up for the loss of war-weary Russia as an ally.

In March and April 1918, Germany attempted to press their advantage of newly available troops from Russia by initiating actions in the Somme and Ypres, the Michael and Georgette offensives, respectively. Both were repulsed by the Allies, in large part due to a more coordinated Allied command structure and their availability to better reinforce and resupply troops from the rear. Indicative of the war's preceding offensives and the callousness to the plight of the poilu in the trenches, German Army pushes that Spring were at the expense of great losses of life on both sides. A third German attempt, the Blucher-Yorck

195   *"1917: The Rage of Men," The History Place, http://www.historyplace.com/worldhistory/ firstworldwar/index-1917.html*

196   *This fear among German commanders became real in November in the ports of Kiel and Wilhelmshaven, where sailors mutinied, refusing to put to sea to fight the British in one last colossal battle.*

Offensive, was wildly successful, but so much so that an over-confident Germany, in its attempt to run for the goal line and capture Paris, again out-paced its logistics and was ultimately repulsed by a consolidated Allied force, including Americans, again almost literally within sight of the City of Lights.

By the Summer of 1918, the German iron had cooled and begun to rust. After three exhausting offensives and three losses, including one near-victory snatched from their hands at almost the last minute, German commanders could see but one inevitable outcome. It became clear that they could not win the war. In an effort to strengthen their hand during inevitable ceasefire negotiations, they attacked twice more, first in a third attempt to capture Paris and then with an offensive against Reims in the Marne. Both advances were blocked by French and American troops.

The Allies became emboldened by their successes. Reinforced with fresh American troops and equipment, they initiated attacks all along the Somme and Marne rivers, with counter-offensives at Amiens in July, Noyon in August, and Saint Mihiel in September. In late September, they turned their sights on the Meuse River, advancing yards at a time for six weeks through the mud-filled craters and rain in the Argonne Forest. Simultaneously, Belgian and British troops pushed back Germany in the Fourth Battle of Ypres and pushed through a 20-mile stretch of the Sigfried Line between Cambrai and St. Quentin. By early October, Germany's Sigfried Line had collapsed. Combined with losses elsewhere around the world – Italy, Turkey, Palestine, and Bulgaria – and facing a likely all-out defeat, German commanders urged Kaiser Wilhiem to sue for peace.

224.

Chapter One: Life after death

"The nightmare is finally over. Planes from the English airfield near us start flying very low as a sign of rejoicing. On the ground, they set fire to several cans of gasoline that flare up; the bonfire lasts all day. The church bells are ringing and in the distance, bugles sound the "cease fire." The war is over.

"The civilians cry for joy. We soldiers prepare a feast to celebrate with dignity the end of this calamity which has held us for four years and taken away many of our parents and our good comrades. At the dinner, we are told the balance of our losses since the foundation of the Company in May 1915. It is terrible to think of all those we knew who will not see their families again. But we who are left can now hope to bring back our skin (sic), unless an accident happens, which is always possible.

"We stay a few more days in the Xirocourt community, which is not a very interesting country. We are in the Meurthe-et-Moselle department, which, like the Meuse, is not always very hospitable to soldiers. The weather is superb, but I think I have caught a flu that could prevent me from going back on leave. I tell Dr. Leferne, who is chief of the mess hall, and he gives me a prescription to be taken to a pharmacy in Nancy, where I have to embark on a train to go on leave anyway. Unofficially, I am supposed to leave with my comrades Bouin and Desecaye on the 14th, but naturally, this is only a rumor in the Company because no soldiers here have yet been granted exceptional leave to visit the Lille area.

"Regardless, I make my preparations to depart. I buy all that I can buy that I think might be needed by my parents. Nancy is 30 kilometers from where we are, so we leave with several soldiers on permission. In Maxéville, we find a truck going to Nancy, succeed in getting a seat, and reach Nancy at 2 o'clock in the afternoon, early enough to run some errands and buy the syrup ordered by the doctor.

"As I walk towards the station, I am now all alone. When I get

(Previous page) French postcard, French infantrymen and British calvary sharing cigarettes. Colorized photograph, by E.L. Deley., Set 201, No. 4., 12th edition. Untitled. Printed by Vise, Paris, Image from card written September 11, 1915, location unknown. Unposted.

there, a small revolution is developing. The soldiers on leave want to take the trains scheduled to leave at once, but our service orders oblige us to only board special trains routed to Favresse, which will take forever. After failing several times to board the right train, I sit down on the footboard of one parked along the track, with my head in my hands, to wait. As nobody came to disturb me, I fell asleep. I woke up to some movement and the train whistle. I felt it start forward, so I delicately raised my feet. And so it was: the train left the station, it was 8 o'clock in the evening, and nobody saw my transgression.

"I must admit, I sat quietly on the footboard in the hope of being able to get into the train compartment at the first station 30 kilometers away, perhaps Lunéville or Lérouville. So as not to risk getting caught during a leave inspection, I mingled in the station and waited for the train to start again. I left the station, and found a seat in a compartment and arrived safely in Paris... where I was scolded by authorities and told that I should not have taken that train. But it was done, and since it was only 3 o'clock in the afternoon, I ran a few errands, then returned to the station early to be sure not to miss my train, after first having dinner, of course. Because it was 7 o'clock in the evening and the train had to leave at 8 o'clock, I was sure to find a seat but many others had the same idea as me and in a very short while the train was full. At exactly 8:50 we left Paris.

"I am going home. What a joy to think that soon I will see my family again, a family that I have not seen since I left Roubaix on October 8, 1914."

On November 11, 1918, Arthur found himself in Xirocourt about a mile west of the Moselle River, 200 miles east of Paris. A hundred or so miles southeast of Verdun, Xirocourt was behind the lines but close to the trenches along France's contested border with Germany.

Although the war ends on page 106 of Arthur's journal, his experiences continue for another 100 pages, about half of his autobiographical notes. Many of the remaining pages include details about each of his leaves, which he refers to as "permissions," and a list of the dead soldiers and officers Arthur personally knew or served with throughout the war.

The last months of summer and the Fall of 1918 saw the

confluence of several strategic storm fronts, whirlwinds of events that led up to the secession of fighting that came to be called "The Armistice."

In August 1918, the Allies, fortified with new, young blood from America, attacked in the Somme with more than 450 tanks. It would be the start of an offensive historians would label "the last 100 days." Germany's great efforts early in the year to take land and perhaps capture Paris disintegrated as thousands of German officers and men surrendered. One German commander on the German General Staff, Colonel Albrecht Their, wrote in his diary of "the black day" for the German Army:

> "We had expected too much from the great effort of March, perhaps even the end of the war. That is why everyone joined together and consolidated their support. Now the deception is there, and it is huge. Our attacks, even when well prepared by artillery, are stopped... inferior troops panic the moment they are hit by losses...there is insufficient artillery." [197]

By September, the Allied counter-offensive led by the British broke through the Hindenburg Line, retaking Graincourt and long contested villages in the Somme. Soon, the Allies secured Arras in the Pas-de-Calais department; Noyon in the Oise, Cambrai in du Nord; St. Quentin in the Aisne, and the Argonne Forest in the Meuse. The British alone captured ten thousand prisoners and two hundred pieces of artillery in the Somme. Once past the trenches, it was open country and by October 19, Lille, Bruges, and Ostende were also once again in Allied hands.

An influenza epidemic, however, complicated war logistics and strategy on both sides, sweeping through Europe in the Fall of 1918. [198] It had started in the late Spring with a three-day

---

197   *The Great War and the Shaping of the 20th Century, Winter & Baggett, pg. 304*

198   *The Great War and the Shaping of the 20th Century, Winter & Baggett, pg. 305*

fever and few deaths, but a fast-acting, vicious, and more virulent strain reemerged in the Fall. Eventually, soldiers and refugees returning home -- soldiers like Arthur, who appers to have caught a light case of it -- spread the virus into a pandemic that by 1919 had killed as many as 40 million people.[199]

On his first day of the war, Arthur left Roubaix with two friends, brothers Paul and Fernand Debruyne, but the three became separated even before they had reached the outskirts of Lille. The older brother, Fernand Henri Debruyne of the 45th Infantry Regiment, born May 29th, 1890, was recorded to have died in an English hospital in Greece on December 11, 1918 of influenza "contractee en service,' or contracted during his time in service. His younger sibling Paul Marius Debruyne of the 87th Infantry Regiment, born in August 1895, died in a military hospital in Dijon, France, on December 20, 1915, of "suites des Blessures de guerre," or complication from wounds received in battle. Also, on that first day of his war, Arthur took up with a coworker, Fernand Masquelier, and together they completed the journey to the induction center in Perigreux. A Fernand Joseph Masquelier, born in November 1896 in Roubaix, of the 8th Battalion de Chasseurs a Pieds, was reported killed by enemy fire on April 10, 1916 in the Meuse. According to records, he was part of the induction Class of 1916, indicating he reapplied to join the Army after being turned down for service in Arthur's Class of 1915. [200]

By all accounts, Charles Boyon, Arthur's best friend, survived the war and received a good conduct discharge and decorations, serving until March 11, 1919. He is recorded to have served in the 27th, 25th and 242nd Regiments of the 8th Infantry.

After the terrible experience at L'Esparges in Verdun in 1915, Craonne in 1916, in Belgium and Flanders from August

199   What started out as a European epidemic soon became a pandemic as soldiers returned to homes around the world. By the time the plague had run its course, it had killed 50 million people, more than died in combat during the war itself. (https://www.archives.gov/exhibits/influenza-epidemic/)

200   All three deaths can be found recorded in France's Grand Memorial Database, http://www.culture.fr/Genealogie/Grand-Memorial

through October 1917, and Vertes Fenilles and La Verte-Milou in May through July 1918, Arthur's 110th Infantry Regiment also fought at the L'Ourcq River in the Marne department at the end of August 1918. During the course of the war, the unit was cited for their valor and their contributions at Verdun (February 21 – September 6, 1916), the Battle of the Somme (September 5-October 5, 1916), the Battle of Flanders (August 16-25, 1917 and again October 9- December 5, 1917), and the Battle of L'Ourcq (July 18-20 August, 1918). Arthur personally was awarded France's War Cross.

While the French soldiers in the trenches may have questioned the wisdom and sanity of the authority that demanded from the poilu such personal sacrifices, few of the infantrymen faulted France and all of them knew the Prussian War-like consequences of an ultimate strategic failure of the cause. They all expected to die, but to varying degrees, every poilu hoped that their sacrifice would help seed a new beginning for France.

Author Peter Hart in his book about the Battle of the Somme summarized both the tragedy of and the overarching lesson from the atrocious death and destruction of five years of global war:

> "Once such as global war had been declared then the future of a generation was handed to cold-hearted military professionals like Sir Douglas Haig, Eric von Falkenhayn and Joseph Joffe. [To them,] The fighting was not futile unless the war was futile. The responsibility for all the manifold sacrifices lies not so much with the generals as with the enthusiasm with which the world embraced war in 1914." [201]

Just as the cause of the war was rooted in a bird's nest of alliances and national self-interests, what brought about a cessation of fighting was a complicated confluence of internal

---

201   *The Somme, Peter Hart, Pegasus Books, NY, pg. 529*

French War Cross, Le Croix de Guerre, with Bronze Star citation, awarded to Arthur Dumoulin for service to France, 1914-1918.

230.

and external factors. In July 1918, the American influence was beginning to be felt and the tide of war was turning against Germany. The German High Command came to the conclusion that they could no longer win the war. Access to natural resources was waning on both sides and Allied port blockades were beginning to starve the German civilian population. A revolution in the East pulled Russia out of the war but French and German leaders feared similar uprisings in their own countries. Germany's Reichstag party, which had proposed an unratified Peace Resolution of 1917, came to power in a change of government. Even as late as October, German military leaders held out the hope of armistice terms that might allow them enough time to reposition their troops and enable Germany to negotiate for peace from a much stronger position. France, too, considered holding out longer for more favorable terms, but French citizens were exhausted from four years of defensive war and public polls were strongly in favor of peace. By the end of October, 1918, it became quite clear at every level: it was time for the fighting to stop. [202]

An armistice was signed by all combatants on November 11, 1918, but it took France well into 1919 to methodically draw down its army and slowly release its soldiers, sailors, and airmen back into civilian life.

If there is a demand to continue Arthur's story beyond Armistice Day, his transition period, and his return to Roubaix, perhaps this book's next edition will include an unabridged transcription and translation as an appendix. For now, however, it is sufficient to simply say: "And then, suddenly, there was peace."

---

202   *The Final Battle: Soldiers of the Western Front and the German Revolution of 1928, Scott Stephenson, Cambridge University Press, Sept 2009, pgs. 115-119.*

Chapter Two: Significance

After more than 100 years of reflection and scholarly study, peppered with lessons from a number of large world, regional, and internal conflicts that erupted following the end of the "war to end all wars," it is safe to say that a country's decision to go to war is so often directly related to two things: its perception of threat and the mindset, intelligence, and ethical point of view of its government's leaders. In both cases, a country's citizens bear the responsibility, either because they elected decision-makers (in a democracy), allowed it to happen (in a monarchy), or succumbed to intimidation (if ruled by a despot).

The decision to go to war cannot be an easy one and, of course, there's no way to know what the outcome will be in advance, only hindsight. The responsibilities and decisions that leaders shoulder are but proxies for the responsibility and decisions that individual citizen and military men and women have given them. By extension, that makes every individual responsible and accountable to some degree for their own fate, the fate of future generations, and in the case of WWI's world-wide chaos.

In Germany, the citizen's pride in the strength of its military reflected the arrogance among its leadership and a nationalistic belief that sheer might would lead to a short and again profitable outcome. Government leaders made little attempt to soften their treaty commitments or otherwise avoid conflict. Kaiser Wilhelm II, either as an advocate for war or by acquiescing to his generals' demand for it, was unquestionably at its epicenter. Precipitating the long and bloody battle for Verdun, German Chief of General Staff von Falkenhayn's stated military objective was to "bleed France white" by taunting the French to throw every soldier necessary into battle to defend a fortress that had little military value but significant national pride. This cavalier

French proof of service combatant card, Arthur Dumoulin, issued circa 1935

perspective cost the French 400,000 casualties at Verdun, but also bled the German army of 350,000 men.

In France, the citizen's desire for revenge, their trust in their military's judgement, and unquestioned sense of duty resulted in an acceptance of absolute, inflexible doctrines of warfare and an acquiescence of France's internal efforts to stamp out the voices of pacifism and descent. To be fair, after the German invasion in 1914 the French government had little choice but to fight unconditionally for its very existence but the fact that French military leaders felt it necessary to arbitrarily select soldiers – innocent or not -- for firing squad executions after the Army's internal uprisings in July 1917 is just one example of the French government's and military leadership's attitudes towards the plight of the individual soldier, justice at the individual level, and their desperate desire to stick to "the plan." It also stands as an example of the hard choices, right or wrong, that leaders are forced to make on behalf of their populace.

Russia's war with Germany on the Eastern Front, although not really addressed in this book, presents a library of examples and lessons about responsibility. Russia opted out of the war, but only after Tsar Nicholas II's armies had loss more than 1.5 million men and his government was overthrown. Like Wilhelm II, Nicholas could have elected a softer response to the Austria-Hungary and Serbian fighting, but he did not.

In the case of Great Britain, there probably was no way to avoid being drawn into the conflict but once engaged, pride in military tradition and faith in traditional battlefield doctrine, and perhaps a lack of creative thinking and flexible strategies on the part of military leaders, contributed to the war's stalemate, as demonstrated by the loss of 56,000 men on the first day of the Battle of the Somme.

The United States waited until 1917 to enter the war and joined the Allies only after years of resistance by Woodrow Wilson and a public outcry over the loss of American lives following German unrestricted submarine attacks and the sinking of the British ocean liner, the Lusitania. Although in reality the U.S. lost more lives in battle than it would have ever lost on the high seas, its citizenry and government weighed the casualty consequences against concepts such as freedom, peace, and democracy and collectively made an educated decision.

The fires of fear and paranoia, stoked by nationalism, weak cross-border communication, unwarranted military confidence, and a cavalier approach to consequences at the individual level – both civilians and soldiers – have lessons even today. As do lessons learned about the cost of individual suffering caused by preemptive actions or military applications of a country's might for the human rights of freedom, peace, equal-say-in- governing (i.e., democracy), and individual expression.

In a smaller way, the WWI combatant's story also parallels that of today's soldiers and those in the recent past who served in

Vietnam, Iran, Afghanistan, Syria, and elsewhere since, and is an example of how PTSD can be bravely faced and overcome with help.

During WWI for the first-time, doctors and staff working to rehabilitate injured soldiers began to recognize "shell shock" as an injury and began to track it in two forms, commotional (physical) and neurasthenia, or stress-related. Today we refer to these as traumatic brain injury (TBI) and post-traumatic stress disorder (PTSD). Prior to WWI, shell shock was seen as primarily stress-related, with only about 10 percent of all cases attributed to actual physical injury. During WWI, however, doctors drawing spinal fluids from patients with shell shock discovered changes in protein cells, linking both TBI and PTSD and establishing the beginnings of a clinical diagnosis. [203]

Today, that diagnosis has evolved into treatment of troops coming off of the fields of battle in such places as Iraq and Afghanistan, where, according to a recent RAND Corporation study, as many as 19 percent of soldiers, about 380,000, may have sustained some form of "shell shock." [204] Today we recognize and treat soldiers for TBI and PTSD, having evolved such treatments and therapies from the many wars that followed WWI. But imagine the number of undiagnosed and untreated French citizen soldiers – not to mention soldiers from all the other combating countries – who suffered the symptoms of "being blown up," a countless number unknowingly suffering for the rest of their lives.

WWI serves as a poster child for the consequences of unfettered military control of decisions for tactical or military strategy during wartime. In 1916, for example, Germany retaliated for Allied decisions to use war prisoners as war labor in North Africa and in French ports to help offload war supplies by transferring French and British POWs to some of its worst camps

---

203   *"The Shock of War," Caroline Alexander, Smithsonian Magazine On-line, September 2010, https://www.smithsonianmag.com/history/the-shock-of-war-55376701/*

204   *ibid*

in the Baltics and along the Eastern Front. [205] The two largest examples of the cost of military expediency, of course, were Germany's sinking of hospital ships and passenger liners like the Lusitania and Wilhelm II leadership of the Russian military. The former led to the United States' entry into the war; the latter resulted in Russia's exit. [206]

Of course, the consequences of the expediency of tactical military decisions over strategic political ones neither started nor ended with WWI, and arguably got worse in the 100 years that followed. Historic examples too numerous to list – then and now – make a compelling case for universal rules of war and against total or unconditional warfare.

When leaders forget that war is but a tool to create a new peacetime paradigm and that every war will eventually end and leave a new reality in its wake, they fail as leaders. WWI provided a number of now classic examples of the impact of long-term political, commercial, or humanitarian consequences. In the case of German decisions, Emperor William II, a weak leader going into the war, was all but controlled by his leading generals, Paul von Hindenburg and Erich Ludendorff [207] so the voices of decent or reason were perhaps too weak or non-existent to make a difference. Regardless, the cost of a decision to initiate war was carried in defeat by Germany and the German people for decades afterwards. For most of the war, Russian decisions were made by Czar Nicholas II, who took charge of the military. As for France, Britain, and the United States, democracies to various degrees under the influence if not control of civilian politicians and bureaucrats, the fault and fallout for wartime decisions lies

---

205 *"Prisoners of War," Heather Jones, https://encyclopedia.1914-1918-online.net/article/prisoners_ of_war*

206 *The logic: inattention to rising domestic unrest led to the Russian Revolution, and eventually Russia's withdrawal from the war.*

207 *"Wilhelm II, German Emperor," https://en.wikipedia.org/wiki/Wilhelm_II,_German_Emperor*

squarely on their shoulders. [208]

Besides learning to deal with such post-war issues like PTSD and post-war political and strategic fallout, the "Great War" changed how countries prepared for war. At the start of the conflict, war was conducted more or less as wars had been carried out for centuries before, with rifles, cannon, sail and steam boats, and horsemen. But a decade before the start of the conflict, new technologies became mainstream, most notably the gas-powered internal combustion engine, and from it, both mass-produced land vehicles and the heavier-than-air craft.

As a consequence, the introduction of new technologies changed the role of the military engineer, and to a great extent, the qualifications of officers and non-commissioned officers. Technology complicated leadership. It was no longer sufficient to want to lead, stepping up to expectations borne of generations of military service as part of a military class. Nor was sheer charisma, brash bravery, or an overwhelming urge to seek glory or honor now enough. No, now more than ever before, leadership required technical knowledge. Brain had replaced heart. [209]

Also, by the end of the war, few French youth aspired to become career soldiers. That life had been lived by millions of Frenchmen and had been found wanting, to say the least. The allure of honor on the battlefield, pennants, and marching bands had been replaced by rotting horse corpses, mud, disease, amputation, and loss. By 1921, France recorded only 9,186 enlistments and 4,289 re-enlistments and by 1926, those numbers had fallen to 5,792 and 3,708, respectively. [210]

Arthur's four-year journey in and out of the trenches could

---

208   *The two largest political strategic failures at the end of war: the Allies decision to impose on Germany humiliating and crippling post-war reparations and economic restrictions and the failure within the United States government to find a compromise that would support Woodrow Wilson's League of Nations initiative. Arguably, both set the scene for an even worst war just twenty years later.*

209   *The French War Machine, Shelby Cullom Davis, George Allen & Unwin, Ltd, 1937, pg. 74*

210   *The French War Machine, Shelby Cullom Davis, George Allen & Unwin, Ltd, 1937, pg. 75*

be considered an example and perhaps an analogue for a number of lessons. Compassion for the individual soldier and individual families shouldn't be, cannot be, lost on military and government leaders. Such issues can have strategic consequences. Also, WWI taught us that sometimes actually executing fixes to perceived problems are far worse than living with the paranoia of as-yet unrealized fears. And, too, wars as horrific as WWI do not necessarily prevent even worse ones.

But there were some positive lessons in the tragedy of WWI and in Arthur's story as well. Individuals can come out alive on the other side of a conflagration like a world war. People can overcome their demonic nightmares and flashbacks -- sometimes struggling with those devils the rest of their lives -- and stubbornly refuse to give into them. And their courage of action and commitment to a better future can inspire generations.

Post-war Arthur, by all accounts was as kind and gentle a soul as can be imagined. His daughter-in-law, Jeanne, described an incident in a favorite restaurant in Lille – perhaps Les Main et Roquette – involving grandfather Arthur, one or two of his children, their spouses, and several grandchildren. One of the grandchildren "of delicate stomach" experienced a bout of projectile vomiting, the kind that comes out of nowhere and can cover a room in an instant. After recovering from the initial surprise, patriarch Arthur, with some panache, is reported to have stood up, folded the four corners of the table cloth over the contents of the table, and walking over to the offending child, picked him up gently, looked him in the eye and simply said "Well, I think we're done here."

Chapter Three:
Postscript and epilogue

"Unfortunately, the truces did not live long: in September after several political maneuvers Hitler used the Cologne agreement as a pretext to invade the Poles. France and England have joined forces and it is a second world war."

"During the Spring nothing spectacular happens, with both camps restraining themselves, but in May the Germans launch a violent offensive with powerful equipment. My French Army is not completely prepared for the war; we move back and again we evacuate. When the confusion starts, Berthe and I decide to leave, taking the children, the 301, [211] and three bicycles. We head down the road to Bethune, but it is so perilous for us that we are forced to return to Roubaix the following day. On Monday, May 21, we try again, this time taking the road to Bray-St. Pol, but by evening we have only come as far as St.-Pol-sur-Ternoise, where we spend the night. Mama being fatigued, we stay a few days, but the Germans are very quickly in control. Foiled, we decide to return to our house, where we will spend the rest of the Occupation."

-- diary entry, Arthur Dumoulin, May 30, 1940

In May, 1940, Adolph Hitler launched his "blitzkrieg," or lightning war, moving swiftly against Holland and Belgium. For Arthur, it was deja vous, bringing back all of the horrors of two decades before. Unlike the patriotic and prideful Arthur of October 1914 on his first day of the war, the premonitions that the Arthur of 1940 must have felt would have been fueled by any latent PTSD he had suppressed. Imagine how frantic but determined he must have been to find a way to keep his family safe.

---

211   *1935 or 1936 Peugeot 301 D Cabriolet*

At first, he tried to take his wife, Berthe, and his three children to Bethune, essentially retracing his first steps into WWI, but this time not as a potential draftee but as a refugee artfully driving his 301 through the crowd like a shepherd splitting his flock. The trunk was full of suitcases and the tools of his trade -- his kitchen knives and sauce pans -- with more boxes on the laps of the car's passengers. Every seat full, a 14-year-old boy named Charles sat in the middle of the back seat, his head higher than everyone else, looking out the window at the young men, just a few years older than he, all walking quickly in small groups, off to enlist. It was reminiscent of what Arthur saw from his café seat in Lille's Grand Place square on the first day of his journey into war a quarter century earlier.

Whether it was due to military activity, weather, panicked crowds, or something else, he does not say, but Arthur was forced to return to Roubaix the next day. He and Berthe tried again, this time making it to Saint-Pol-sur-Ternoise, about 80 km, or 60 miles, southeast of Roubaix, but their efforts defeated, they turned back once more.

At the writing of this late addition to his diary, Arthur would have been 45, the first few sentences having been penned in September 1939. Across the five years of his WWI journal, soldier Arthur wrote from a young man's day-to-day, tactical perspective. He left the grand strategy picture to learned scholars and military generals. The Arthur of 1939, a battle-scared, middle-aged, world-traveled Arthur, however, now writes from a broader, strategic point of view. He refers to "the Germans," not the Boch. He mentions the Cologne agreement, a British concession after the war to withdraw troops from the Cologne region if Germany agreed not to rearm its military. [212] Perhaps more importantly, he

212   The Lights that Failed: European International History, 1919-1933, Zara S. Steiner, Oxford University Press, 2005, pg 247

recognizes that indeed, a second world war had begun.

The strategic Arthur of 1939, if not a world traveler, was more accurately an Atlantic Ocean-traveler. Shortly after the First World War ended, Arthur married Berthe, the middle sister of Paul and Fernand Debruyne. She was a year older than he, and apparently a romance had bloomed during Arthur's visits to Paris in 1917 and 1918. In 1920, the couple had their first child, Paulette. Arthur and Berthe opened a small butcher and catering business in Roubaix but in 1922, Arthur was offered what he considered the opportunity of a lifetime: a chef position in l'Estates-Unis, the United States.

The couple sold or gave their holdings to family or friends, registered through Ellis Island in New York City, and

Food cart, "Dumoulin & Debruyne Catering, Pork Butcher and Cooking," circa 1920

eeentually settelled in Philadelphia, Pennsylvania.

Their middle-class life in Philadelphia was pleasant, and soon the family added son Charles and daughter Denise. But Berthe missed her more familiar France, where there remained a substantial network of family ties and friends. [213] Arthur and Berthe returned via steamship, but unlike the first trip in steerage, Arthur and his family re-crossed the Atlantic in first class accommodations. With the money they'd saved in America, they purchased land in Lys-lez-Lannoy, a community just east of Roubaix, parceling it so that they could build a house on half of it.

---

213   *As reported by Sylvette Ponthieu- Dumoulin, Arthur's granddaughter*

Dumoulin family passport, return trip to France, 1927

The fact that the house resembled what they had lived in in Philadelphia may be an indication of how much they actually enjoyed their several years abroad. Outside, the entry to their new home in Roubaix was marked by an elevated entryway of brick steps; inside it sported every new comfort feature available in a modern American home at the time. Arthur's and Berthe's daughter Paulette was to report later that her father was proud to be one of the first to install central heating and a bathroom with a large bathtub. [214]

In 1943, amidst an army of occupying German soldiers, a large photograph of General Charles de Gaulle is rumored to have hung in the hall, a portrait removed and discreetly tucked away in a closet when guests dropped by.

Eventually, Arthur and Berth built or purchased in Roubaix a line of ten small row houses, which they rented out. But the war years were hard and sometime in 1945, Arthur took on additional work as a cook in a large factory in Seclin, ten miles away. Berthe worked in the factory's canteen, where the workers took their meals. During the week, the family lived in Seclin, but returned to Roubaix on weekends. After the war they moved back to Roubaix permanently, but Arthur's son, Charles Lucian, having been born in Philadelphia, soon exercised his American citizenship and joined the U.S. Army Air Corps. [215]

In 1960, Arthur and Berthe built a second house on the other half of the land they had purchased upon their return to France from America. But as manufacturing began to move offshore throughout northern France, the factory in Seclin closed, putting Arthur, now in his sixties, out of work. For a time, he served as a "candelier," holding eggs up to a strong light to ensure they weren't fertilized and thus good enough to sell, but this work did not last long. He held various jobs as

---

214   *Also reported by Sylvette Ponthieu- Dumoulin, granddaughter*

215   *Charles Lucian retired from the U.S. armed forces, serving 22 years as a military photographer.*

gardener and handyman. Eventually, Arthur returned to being a landlord, and he and Berthe made enough money from the rent of their two houses to build a modest third home, where they lived to the end of their days. [216]

Against all odds, Arthur died quietly in his bed in 1976 at the age of 82.

---

216   *per Sylvette Ponthieu- Dumoulin*

Arthur "sur la divan," (on the sofa), photo by son Charles, 1957

Acknowledgments
and additional explanation

Arthur carried his journal across four years of war: it is amazing that it survived the cold winters, moisture, and mud that he describes within it. The diary must have experienced a thousand miles of foot, mule, and train travel, jostled in the bottom of a dark rucksack. Judging from its clean, unstained pages, the journal was brought out and amended only in relative quiet hours and safer conditions while Arthur was "in reserve status" or "on permission."

The beautifully hand-scripted words, penned in black ink that has faded to red and yellow in places, are barely visible now 100 years later. The book itself, a delicate and literally war-torn, horse glue-bound notebook of 200 thin parchment pages, had to be pulled apart, conserved, and carefully copied before it could be handled by translators.

The effort to transcribe and then translate the journal began long before translation technology was commercially available. Translators had to make sense of context, slang, and the names of villages and people long since lost to history. Special thanks to Francoise Wackenhut and her father for their French-to-English interpretation and research, especially with the first half of the diary.

You can expect to read more about Arthur's son, U.S. airman and military photographer Charles Lucian Dumoulin, in the soon-to-be-published biography/memoir, "The Threads that Bind."

Arthur's descendants in France helped tremendously with the research of the book. Sylvette Ponthieu-Dumoulin provided much of the background about Arthur's ancestry and post-WWI life in Roubaix. Simon Langlet, Arthur's great-grandson in France, spent much time and effort coordinating with his uncles and cousins attempting to pull out facts and photos, and corroborate research.

I would be remiss if I didn't also acknowledge the help of the Archives Salle d'Etudes in Roubaix, archives@ville-roubaix.fr, for their long-distance help finding, pulling, and sending copies of certificates and records. Many thanks, too, to SYSTRANet, a free online translation service, and to other commercial translation services, for help with the second half of the journal and to cross-validate meaning and context.

In many places, Arthur didn't reference dates, and events that took place across many days are separated only by a string of commas and phrases placed in a single sentence. Often, he left only clues to whether an event involved just his squad, a part of his company or regiment, or engaged his whole division. Only rarely did he attribute actions to specific military units or officers. Many thanks in advance to the reader, especially any military historians, who find inconsistences between Arthur's journal and other published works and who then flag these inaccuracies or translation mistakes so that any errors can be corrected in future editions of the book.

-- J. Michael Dumoulin

Ingram Content Group UK Ltd.
Milton Keynes UK
UKHW050744080623
422852UK00005B/7